W9-BMT-647

H A T E
CRIMES

A Reference Handbook

Other Titles in ABC-CLIO's
CONTEMPORARY
WORLD ISSUES
Series

Books in the Contemporary World Issues series address vital issues in today's society such as terrorism, sexual harassment, homelessness, AIDS, gambling, animal rights, and air pollution. Written by professional writers, scholars, and nonacademic experts, these books are authoritative, clearly written, up-to-date, and objective. They provide a good starting point for research by high school and college students, scholars, and general readers, as well as by legislators, businesspeople, activists, and others.

Each book, carefully organized and easy to use, contains an overview of the subject; a detailed chronology; biographical sketches; facts and data and/or documents and other primary-source material; a directory of organizations and agencies; annotated lists of print and nonprint resources; a glossary; and an index.

Readers of books in the Contemporary World Issues series will find the information they need in order to better understand the social, political, environmental, and economic issues facing the world today.

H A T E
CRIMES

A Reference Handbook

Donald Altschiller

CONTEMPORARY
WORLD ISSUES

ABC-CLIO

Santa Barbara, California
Denver, Colorado
Oxford, England

Library of Congress Cataloging-in-Publication Data
Altschiller, Donald.
    Hate crimes : a reference handbook / Donald Altschiller.
        p. cm.—(Contemporary world issues)
    ISBN 0-87436-937-1 (alk. paper)
    1. Hate crimes—United States.   I. Title.   III. Series.
HV6773.52.A47   1999
364.1—dc21   98-50275
                                                                CIP

05 04 03 02 01 00 99   10 9 8 7 6 5 4 3 2 1

ABC-CLIO, Inc.
130 Cremona Drive, P.O. Box 1911
Santa Barbara, California 93116–1911

This book is printed on acid-free paper ∞ .

Manufactured in the United States of America

Contents

Preface

As a teenager, I once walked past a playground pretty far from my home where many tough-looking kids were congregated. Soon, they started screaming at me that no Puerto Ricans were welcome in their neighborhood (although those were not their precise words). Suddenly, two of them jumped me, threw me to the ground and proceeded to beat me. Finally, I was able to wrest myself away from them and ran a long way home, bloody and aching.

As it turns out, I'm not Puerto Rican. Nor do I think it would have helped if I had told those thugs that I was Jewish. This senseless violence was once considered mere teenage hooliganism. Now, it is appropriately labeled a hate crime.

The term "hate crime" is of very recent vintage. According to NYU law professor James B. Jacobs, the phrase first appeared in the media in 1985, with eleven articles on hate crime published in newspapers throughout the country. By less than a decade later, more than 1,000 articles covered the topic.

Throughout American history, hate crimes have been a persistent and, occasionally, widespread phenomena. Different terms have been used to describe these crimes, such as lynching, church burning or synagogue vandalism, and police brutality, to name only a few.

This book, I hope, will provide students, lawyers, scholars, journalists, and researchers a detailed overview on the current problem of hate crimes in the United States and the various responses of law enforcement officials, the legislative and judicial branches of government, and community groups in dealing with this issue. Although my research has personally convinced me about the importance of and need for hate crimes legislation, I have included much material which raises legal, philosophical, sociological, and political objections to these laws. This book aims to inform and educate the student and researcher about the complexities of this social problem.

The first section surveys the recent history of hate crimes legislation and describes the most frequently victimized racial, religious, and other groups, including the nature and type of incidents they suffer.

The second section provides a chronology of hate crimes since the beginning of the modern civil rights movement. In compiling this section, I have spent a considerable amount of time attempting to find the names of the victims. Hate crimes not only inflict physical harm but also demean an individual as a mere faceless member of a social category. "A black is lynched" or "two gay persons were murdered" are the type of reported descriptions that denude the victims of their humanity. By listing the names of these victims, my fervent hope is that at least the perpetrators will not succeed in this aspect of their hateful activities. Regrettably, I have not been able to locate the names of all the victims listed.

The third section includes brief biographies of notable individuals involved in the study and/or control and prevention of hate crimes. The next section includes many important primary sources: Among these documents are the texts of legislation, judicial decisions, and national and state hate crime reports. In addition, I have included excerpts from manuals and testimonies of nongovernmental agencies that help organize community responses to fight hate crimes.

The fifth section is a detailed directory of national and local organizations dedicated to promoting tolerance and monitoring extremist groups. The last two chapters provide important bibliographic information—print and nonprint—on many aspects of hate crimes. These sections, I believe, contain the most comprehensive listing of sources currently available on this topic.

During my long friendship with Bob Frankel, I have had many discussions on these and related matters. His remarkable knowledge and eclectic interests have enhanced this work. I cherish his friendship.

A book on such an unpleasant topic does not easily lend itself to a dedication. My precious wife Ellen always inspires my dedication and love.

Donald Altschiller

Introduction 1

O n June 18, 1984, Alan Berg, a popular Denver radio talk show host, was murdered in a machine gun attack in the driveway of his home. His assailants—members of a neo-Nazi group—were convicted three years later of murder. According to trial testimony, the murderers stalked him for several days because they were enraged by his frequent on-air attacks against white supremacists and neo-Nazis. "They killed him because of his job, and they did it because he was a Jew," asserted Thomas O'Rourke, an assistant U.S. attorney.

More than a decade later, on December 7, 1995, Michael James and Jackie Burden were murdered in Fayetteville, North Carolina, by soldiers from nearby Fort Bragg. The two African Americans were randomly selected by the soldiers, who had strong ties with white supremacist organizations. Only a month later, on January 29, 1996, Thien Minh Ly, a 24-year-old Vietnamese American male in Tustin, California, was kicked, stomped, and stabbed more than a dozen times by two white males. A subsequent investigation found the assailants also had a long history of involvement with racist and neo-Nazi groups.

Although these tragic incidents are relatively rare, they nevertheless represent a disturbing phenomenon—the occurrence of hate crimes in the United States.

What is a hate crime? How does it differ from other crimes directed at individuals or property? According to the Federal Bureau of Investigation (FBI), a hate crime is a "criminal offense committed against a person or property that is motivated in whole or in part by the offender's bias against a race, religion, ethnic/national origin group or sexual orientation group." In short, hate crimes are directed against members of a specific group largely because of their membership in that particular group.

Hate crimes occur in different forms and against a variety of particular groups: a swastika scrawled on a grave in a Jewish cemetery; racist and threatening telephone messages against African Americans; physical assaults against gay men and lesbians. In some instances (like those cited earlier), hate crimes result in the deadliest form of violence: murder.

Most people would agree that hate crimes are odious criminal actions. But should they be punished differently from other criminal activities? Advocates of hate crime legislation directly address the rationale for special punishment. "Harm caused by violence that is motivated by bias can be greater than the harm done by ordinary acts involving the same amount of violence," writes Columbia University law professor Kent Greenawalt in the 1992–1993 volume of the *Annual Survey of American Law.* He continues, "The victim may suffer special injury because he or she is aware that race is the basis for an attack. Such crimes can frighten and humiliate other members of the community; they can also reinforce social divisions and hatred. For our society at this time, crimes of bias present particular dangers. That is a sufficient justification in principle to warrant special treatment under the criminal law."

Some Major Targeted Groups

Although the multicultural nature of American society enriches the lives of its citizens, the diversity of cultures and ethnic groups has unfortunately also evoked resentment and hatred among some individuals. Throughout American history and in recent times, many groups have been targets of this hatred, including Irish Catholic immigrants, South American refugees, Arab shopkeepers, Muslim students, and non-English speakers. The number of groups hate crimes have touched is indeed too large to enumerate.

This section surveys the recent history of hatred and violence against four groups that are historically and—according to FBI annual hate crime statistics—most frequently targeted: African Americans, Jewish Americans, gay men and lesbians, and Asian Americans.

African Americans

Violence against black Americans has a long and tragic history in the United States, starting with slavery and continuing with lynchings, firebombings, cross burnings, and assassinations. From 1882 to 1968, a reported 4,743 people were lynched; of those, the vast majority were black. In 1882, 200 known lynchings occurred in a single year.

"Anti-black violence has been and still remains the prototypical hate crime," according to the on-line report *Hate Crimes in America* by the Leadership Conference Education Fund. "Hate crimes against African Americans impact upon the entire society not only for the hurt they cause but for the history they recall and perpetuate." (This report, which also covers several other groups, is available on the Internet at the following web site: http:// www.civilrights.org/lcef/hate.toc.html)

The FBI's *Hate Crime Statistics*, 1996, reported the following breakdown on hate crimes by race:

- Total incidents—8,759
- Attacks against individual blacks—4,600
- Attacks against individual whites—1,445
- Number of known offenders
  - White—5,891 (66 percent)
  - Black—1,826 (20 percent)

In recent years, the most publicized incidents have been the burning of African American churches in the South. In June 1996, President Bill Clinton established the National Church Arson Task Force (NCATF) to better coordinate the efforts of federal, state, and local law enforcement. The NCATF has opened investigations into 670 arsons, bombings, and attempted bombings that occurred at houses of worship between January 1, 1995, and September 8, 1998. Since January 1995, federal, state, and local authorities have arrested 308 suspects in connection with the investigation. Of the 308 persons arrested, 254, or 82 percent, are white and 46, or 14.9 percent, are black. Of the 106 suspects arrested for arsons at African American churches, 64 percent are white and 34 percent are black. Of the 197 arrested at non–African American houses of worship, 91 percent are white, 4 percent are black, and 4 percent are Hispanic. The report issued by the NCATF asserts that the arsons at both African American and other houses of worship "were motivated by a wide array of factors, including not only blatant racism or religious hatred but also financial profit, burglary, and personal revenge." (The full report is available on the Internet at the following web site: http://www. atf.treas.gov/pub/arson98.htm)

Although the report findings do not point to a national conspiracy against black churches, this widespread criminal violence warrants the concern of law enforcement officials and the American public. "If it is not a conspiracy," warned an Anti-Defamation League publication, *Hate Crimes Laws 1998,* "it only means that individuals in different parts of the country at different times, often inspired by hate, are acting independently to commit these crimes."

Although newspapers and the electronic media printed and broadcast extensive reports about the "epidemic" of church bombings, it wasn't until *USA Today* published a three-day series of twelve articles from June 28–30, 1996, that the exact nature of these crimes was examined in detail. However, investigative journalist Michael Fumento, writing in the *Wall Street Journal* (July 8, 1996), argued that *USA Today* was partially responsible for wrongly positing, in his view, an epidemic of fires against African American churches.

Epidemic or not, attacks against black churches have a long track record: according to historian C. Eric Lincoln, the first recorded arson against a black church took place in South Carolina in 1822. After the Civil War, the Ku Klux Klan targeted black churches; almost a century later, four black children were killed in the 16th Street Baptist Church bombing in Birmingham, Alabama, in 1963.

"In our society, arson of a church attended predominantly by African Americans carries a unique and menacing threat that these individuals are physically vulnerable because of their race," testified Deval Patrick, assistant attorney general for civil rights, before the U.S. House of Representatives Committee on the Judiciary on May 21, 1996.

Other notable hate crimes against blacks in the past two decades include:

- On the night of August 20, 1980, Joseph Paul Franklin, a 39-year-old former member of the Ku Klux Klan and American Nazi Party, murdered two black men as they jogged alongside two white women in a Salt Lake City park. Franklin later admitted from his prison cell that he had committed the murders because he was against "race mixing." Franklin was later connected to other crimes, including the bombing of a synagogue in Chattanooga, Tennessee, and shooting Vernon E. Jordan, former head of the National Urban League.

- On March 21, 1981, Michael Donald, a 19-year-old African American, was lynched by United Klans of America members in Mobile, Alabama. The Southern Poverty Law Center filed a lawsuit against the Klan, and in February 1987 an Alabama jury found the Klan liable for Donald's death. His mother was awarded $7 million in damages.

- "There's niggers on the boulevard. Let's kill them," shouted a teenager to his companions in the predominantly white neighborhood of Howard Beach, New York, on December 20, 1986. After being beaten by his pursuers, Michael Griffith, a 23-year-old African American, desperately tried to escape by running across a major thoroughfare but was immediately struck by a car and killed. His stepfather, Cedric Sandiford, was severely beaten with bats, a tire iron, and a tree stump.

- On November 13, 1988, Mulugeta Seraw, an Ethiopian immigrant, was beaten to death by white skinheads in Portland, Oregon. On behalf of the Seraw family, the Southern Poverty Law Center and the Anti-Defamation League (ADL) filed a wrongful death suit against Tom Metzger and his group, White Aryan Resistance, who were charged with instigating and encouraging the violence. On October 22, 1990, an Oregon jury ordered Metzger, his son, and their organization to pay more than $8 million in damages to the Seraw family.

- On March 29, 1996, soon after Bridget Ward and her two daughters had moved to the white working-class neighborhood of Bridesburg in Philadelphia, Pennsylvania, she found racial slurs smeared on her house and received antiblack taunts from some neighbors. After receiving a letter threatening her family, she moved back to her former neighborhood in north Philadelphia. This incident, which was covered by the national media, created citywide concern about the prevalence of antiblack racism in Philadelphia.

Jewish Americans

Anti-Semitism has a pernicious history throughout the ages and around the world. In fact, a 1991 British Thames television documentary series on the subject was aptly titled *The Longest Hatred.* In the United States too, anti-Jewish hatred and violence has flared periodically.

Probably the most notorious anti-Jewish incident in the United States during the twentieth century occurred in Atlanta, Georgia. Leo Frank, the Jewish part-owner of a pencil factory, was wrongfully accused of murdering a 14-year-old employee, Mary Phagan. In July 1915, a mob lynched Leo Frank, encouraged by widespread community anger and the anti-Jewish invective of Tom Watson, a Southern populist politician. This murder stirred immense fear among Southern Jews, precipitating an exodus of Jews from the region.

Despite this incident and the rise of anti-Jewish hatemongers like Father Coughlin, Gerald L. K. Smith, and pro-Nazi groups during World War II, the virus of anti-Semitism has fortunately never exhibited a major strain in American life. "No decisive event, no deep crisis, no powerful social movement, no great individual is associated primarily . . . with anti-Semitism (in America)," wrote historian John Higham.

Nevertheless, anti-Jewish incidents continue to occur, ranging from swastika spray paintings at synagogues and Jewish cemeteries to harassment, intimidation, and violent assaults. In recent years, the most serious anti-Jewish incident occurred in the Crown Heights neighborhood of Brooklyn, New York, following a traffic accident. On August 19, 1991, the driver of a car that was part of a motorcade for Rabbi Menachem M. Schneerson (the spiritual leader of the Lubavitcher Hasidic movement) accidentally hit Gavin Cato, a seven-year-old African American boy, and his cousin Angela, resulting in his death and the injury of his cousin. A riot ensued over the following three days, during which crowds roamed the streets yelling, "Get the Jews." Jewish homes, cars, and property were attacked. On the night of the accident, 20 black youths assaulted Yankel Rosenbaum, an Australian Jewish scholar, stabbing him and leaving him bleeding on an automobile hood. He later died.

On March 1, 1994, Rashid Baz, a Lebanese immigrant, shot at a van carrying fifteen Hasidic Jewish students over the Brooklyn Bridge. One student, 16-year-old Aaron Halberstam, died in the attack. Three other students were wounded; one of them, 18-year-old

Nachum Sasonkin, lost his hearing in one ear and now has trouble walking. The murderer once vowed to "kill all Jews."

In another violent incident, a Jewish store owner in Harlem wanted to expand his clothing store, Freddy's Fashion Mart, to a space then occupied by a black-owned record establishment. The owner of the record store didn't want to move, and some community activists supported his decision. For several weeks, they picketed Freddy's Fashion Mart, occasionally shouting anti-Jewish slurs and rhetoric, including the term "bloodsuckers"—a phrase that Nation of Islam leader Louis Farrakhan used only a few weeks earlier to describe Jews in a widely publicized interview. On December 8, 1995, Roland Smith, one of the protesters, entered the store brandishing a revolver and shot four people. He then doused the premises with lighter fluid. Eight people—including the gunman/arsonist—died in the blaze. Although none of the victims were Jewish, anti-Jewish hatred was nevertheless an underlying factor of the crime.

According to recent FBI *Hate Crime Statistics* tabulations, the overwhelming majority of attacks upon individuals or institutions because of their religion—averaging approximately 85 percent of these targeted crimes annually—were directed against Jewish Americans.

Since 1979, the Anti-Defamation League has published an annual survey of anti-Jewish hate incidents throughout the United States. According to the 1996 *Audit of Anti-Semitic Incidents,* 781 acts of vandalism occurred that year, a 7-percent increase over 1995; acts of harassment, threat or assault, however, declined 16 percent to 941 from a 1995 total of 1,116. In 1996, 12 attacks against Jewish cemeteries were reported; such attacks average about 20 per year over the past five years.

Among the most serious incidents in 1996 were:

• On July 9, 1996, two men shot a BB gun inside a Milwaukee synagogue during morning prayers.
• In September 1996, sixty grave markers were toppled at the Bikur Cholim Sheveth Cemetery in East Haven, Connecticut.
• On November 11, 1996 (the night following the anniversary of *Kristallnacht,* the infamous rampage against Jews in Nazi Germany in 1938), two Arizona synagogues in Phoenix and Tucson were attacked. A Molotov cocktail was thrown at one synagogue but didn't explode, causing only minor damage.

The 1996 *Audit* indicated that 66 incidents ended in arrests by law enforcement agencies. "While this may seem like a small number," states the report, "it is important to remember that not all incidents constitute crimes. Of the incidents that are crimes, the vast majority are anonymous vandalism incidents, often difficult for police to solve."

The ADL statistics are "far more than just numbers on a page," the report wisely notes. "Each statistic tells a story of a community in outrage, a family in fear or a person feeling humiliated and powerless by hate directed at them not for their actions, but for their religion. This open affront to a person's religious identity and personal dignity leaves an indelible scar, which can remain with them for life." Through its various programs, especially the WORLD OF DIFFERENCE Institute, the Anti-Defamation League helps to educate students, teachers, law enforcement officials, and the general community about the importance of encouraging tolerance and respecting differences in our multicultural society.

Gay Men and Lesbians

In a 1988 case involving the beating death of a gay man, a Broward County, Florida, circuit judge jokingly asked the prosecuting attorney, "That's a crime now, to beat up a homosexual?" The prosecutor replied, "Yes, sir. And it's also a crime to kill them." The judge reportedly replied, "Times have really changed" (Valerie Jenness, *Hate Crimes: New Social Movements and the Politics of Violence,* 1997, p. 50).

Prior to the passage of the Hate Crime Statistics Act in 1990, no federal statute addressed the problem of antigay violence. Similarly, very few laws at the state and local level specifically addressed these type of crimes. Only recently has violence against male homosexuals and lesbians been considered a hate crime by the federal government and by most state and local law enforcement agencies. Despite a tide of new legislation concerning the issue, the number of reported crimes against gays has continued to increase.

On October 9, 1986, the U.S. House of Representatives Judiciary Subcommittee on Criminal Justice convened the first congressional hearings on antigay violence throughout the United States. Physicians, psychologists, sociologists, and other health professionals offered testimony on the nature, extent, and consequences of antigay violence.

The first national study focusing exclusively on the topic of antigay violence was conducted by the National Gay and Lesbian Task Force in 1984. Interviewing almost 1,500 gay men and 654 lesbians in eight U.S. cities (Boston, New York, Atlanta, St. Louis, Denver, Dallas, Los Angeles, and Seattle), the respondents reported the following:

- 19 percent reported having been punched, hit, kicked, or beaten at least once in their lives because of their sexual orientation.
- 44 percent had been threatened with physical violence.
- 92 percent of the individuals who were targets of antigay verbal abuse had experienced such harassment "more than once or many times."

(Gregory M. Herek and Kenneth T. Berrill, *Hate Crimes: Confronting Violence Against Lesbians and Gay Men,* 1992, pp. 19–25)

These survey results also highlight another issue involving bias crimes against homosexuals: statistics on antigay crimes vary greatly in reports issued by gay rights activists and law enforcement authorities. In 1992, for example, 421 bias crimes against gay men and lesbians were reported to Minnesota gay rights groups, but only 30 incidents were recorded by Minnesota police. During 1995, the National Coalition of Anti-Violence Programs recorded 2,212 attacks on gay men and lesbians; the FBI, however, cited 1,019 incidents and 1,266 offenses in its 1995 *Hate Crime* report. (Further information and statistics can be found on the Internet site at the following address: http://www.civil-rights.org/lcef/hate/p10.html#B)

When comparing the FBI figures with nongovernmental monitoring groups, it is important to remember that the private organizations have been monitoring hate crimes for a longer period of time than has the government. Whereas the FBI issued its first *Hate Crime* report in 1991, the National Gay and Lesbian Task Force (NGLTF) has been conducting annual surveys of antihomosexual violence since 1985. From 1985 to 1989, the NGLTF gathered statistics from a wide range of community groups and media sources. Since 1990, these reports focus on major metropolitan areas, including Boston, Chicago, Denver, Minneapolis, St. Paul, New York City, and San Francisco.

Gay rights organizations have consistently claimed that antihomosexual hate crimes are vastly underreported, citing several factors. Primary among them is that lesbians and gay men are frequently reluctant to report these incidents, fearing that such publicity would adversely affect their employment or relations with family members unaware of their sexual orientation.

"While victims may want to prosecute their assailants, they are too vulnerable as homosexuals in American society to be exposed in this manner," asserts law scholar Teresa Eileen Kibelstis. She cites a 1994 incident in Los Angeles where eight men were arrested for assaulting two others with baseball bats. Although the police termed the incident "a gay bashing" and arrested the assailants with the aid of witnesses, the victims quickly left the scene of the crime and were never located. "Gay bashing crimes involve gay victims, and for some lesbians and gay men, that label can have too many repercussions," Kibelstis concludes (*Notre Dame Journal of Law, Ethics & Public Policy* 9, 1, 1995).

In addition, gays and lesbians have had troubled relationships with police departments nationwide, both historically and in recent times. The Stonewall riot at a gay bar in New York's Greenwich Village in 1969—considered the founding event in the birth of the modern gay liberation movement—involved a police assault against homosexual men. In recent years, the San Francisco-based Community United Against Violence reported that from January 1984 to March 1986, physical assault by law enforcement officers constituted from 4 to 17 percent of reported antigay incidents (Gary Comstock, *Violence Against Lesbians and Gay Men*, 1991, pp. 152–162). Such incidents are often not recorded in reports by local law enforcement agencies.

Violent hate crimes committed against gays and lesbians are also notable in another respect: these incidents are especially brutal. According to one study, "an intense rage is present in nearly all homicide cases involving gay male victims. A striking feature . . . is their gruesome, often vicious nature. Seldom is the homosexual victim simply shot. He is more apt to be stabbed a dozen or more times, mutilated, and strangled." A hospital official in New York City remarked, "Attacks against gay men were the most heinous and brutal I encountered . . . They frequently involved torture, cutting, mutilation . . . showing the absolute intent to rub out the human being because of his (sexual) preference" (Anthony S. Winer, *Harvard Civil Rights-Civil Liberties Law Review*, Summer 1994).

Recent murders of homosexuals include the following incidents:

• In May 1988, a lesbian couple, Rebecca Wright and Claudia Brenner, were victims of a gruesome murder in Pine Grove State Park in Pennsylvania. The murderer, Stephen Ray Carr, was convicted of first-degree murder and sentenced to life imprisonment.

• Also that month, a college freshman committed a grisly murder of two gay men, Tom Trible and Lloyd Griffen, in a Dallas, Texas, neighborhood. Although the prosecutor requested life imprisonment for the murderer, Richard Lee Bednarski, the trial judge imposed a 30-year sentence and callously declared, "I put prostitutes and gays at about the same level and I'd be hard put to give somebody life for killing a prostitute" (*New York Times*, December 17, 1988, p. 8).

• A Vietnam War veteran, James Zappalorti, was brutally beaten in Staten Island, New York, on January 21, 1990. The murderers, Phillip Sarlo and Michael Taylor, later defiantly declared that they had "only killed a gay" (*Newsday*, November 4, 1990, p. 8).

• On October 27, 1992, Seaman Allen Schindler, while serving on a U.S. Navy ship stationed in Japan, was murdered outside his base. The assailant, Navy Airman Terry Helvey, who had recently learned of Schindler's homosexuality, stomped on his face and chest with his feet. Schindler's body was so disfigured by the brutal murder that seasoned Navy medics were sickened by the vicious nature of the attack.

• On October 6, 1998, Matthew Shepard, a 22-year-old gay student at the University of Wyoming, was lured from a local bar by two men, kidnapped, beaten with a .357 Magnum, and tied to a wooden ranch fence. He hung for almost 18 hours until a passing bicyclist noticed his bloodied body. He lay in a coma in a hospital in Fort Collins, Colorado, until he died on October 12.

In 1995, the New York City Gay and Lesbian Anti-Violence Project reported at least 29 gay-related murders (where sexual orientation was a significant motivating factor) throughout the United States; the project reported 21 such homicides in 1996. The FBI, however, recorded only two murders nationally in 1996 involving sexual orientation bias. Sharen Shaw Johnson of Gay Men and Lesbians Opposing Violence in Washington, D.C. (P.O. Box 34622, Washington, DC 20005), said her organization counted at least two murders in Prince George's County, Maryland, alone (*Washington Blade*, January 16, 1998).

The FBI annual report on hate crimes in the United States placed the number of antigay incidents at 1,016 for 1996, compared to 1,019 in 1995. According to the report, the number of antigay incidents constituted 11 percent of the total of 8,759 reported crimes. As noted earlier, gay rights groups believe these figures are gross underestimates.

The FBI breaks down the antigay crimes in 1996 in this way:

- 757 (75 percent) were antimale homosexual
- 150 (15 percent) were antifemale homosexual
- The remaining crimes were general "antihomosexual" or "antibisexual"

This breakdown was similar to the 1995 report.

As of July 1998, only 21 states and the District of Columbia have passed hate crime laws that include sexual orientation as a protected class. Some states, such as Texas, have deliberately vague language, not specifying any victim group because many conservative legislators refuse to support any protection for homosexuals (*New York Times*, August 30, 1994, p. A15).

Nevertheless, the scope and nature of antigay violence is severe throughout the nation. Although many gay rights advocates acknowledge that any American has the constitutional right to believe that homosexual behavior is immoral or can individually refrain from associating with gay men or lesbians, the issue of violence against gays must have legal and criminal sanctions. "The response that is urgently needed now," write Gregory Herek and Kevin Berrill, "is for public officials, educators, clergy and all people of conscience to condemn . . . antigay violence" (Herek and Berrill, *Hate Crimes: Confronting Violence Against Lesbians and Gay Men*, p. 40).

Asian Americans

In a legal brief filed in the landmark Supreme Court case *Wisconsin v. Mitchell*, the National Asian Pacific American Legal Consortium asserted that Asians rank fourth on the list of victims of hate crimes, behind African Americans, Jews, and gay men and lesbians. Although this ranking may vary from year to year, anti-Asian hate crimes have increased in recent times.

Probably the most notorious and publicized incident in recent decades occurred on June 19, 1982, when a Chinese American was murdered by two laid-off auto workers in Detroit,

Michigan. After provoking a barroom scuffle, Ronald Ebens and his stepson, Michael Nitz, shouted at Vincent Chin, a 27-year-old draftsman—who they believed was Japanese—"It's because of you . . . that we're out of work." The white men then chased him out of the bar and bludgeoned him into a comatose state with a baseball bat. Four days later, Vincent Chin died.

The case received national attention when the judge placed the assailants on probation and required them to pay only a $3,750 fine. Later, Ebens was convicted and Nitz acquitted of civil rights violations. In July 1987, Ebens agreed to pay $1.5 million to Chin's estate to settle a wrongful death damage suit.

"This attack stands out as a perverse symbol of racist violence," asserted an article in the June 1993 issue of the *Harvard Law Review* (no author listed, "Racial Violence Against Asian Americans"). "Even if one presumes that their unemployment was caused by unjust trade practices of the Japanese government . . . they transferred blame not only from the Japanese government to the Japanese people, not only from the Japanese people to United States citizens of Japanese descent, but finally from Japanese Americans to anyone unlucky enough to bear Asian features."

Subsequent heinous murders against Asian Americans have not attracted the national outrage of the Vincent Chin killing:

• In September 1987, a Jersey City gang called "Dot Busters" savagely beat to death Navroze Mody, an Asian Indian American.

• In July 1989, two white men in Raleigh, North Carolina, murdered Ming Hai "Jim" Loo, a 24-year-old Chinese American, attacking him with a gun and a broken bottle. The men later declared that they did not like "Orientals."

• In August 1990, two skinheads shouting "white power" murdered Hung Truong, a 15-year-old Vietnamese youth in Houston, Texas.

• On January 29, 1996, Thien Minh Ly, a Vietnamese man, was kicked, stomped on, and stabbed more than a dozen times by two white supremacists on a tennis court in Tustin, California.

The National Asian Pacific American Legal Consortium (NAPALC), a nonprofit organization whose mission is to advance and protect the legal and civil rights of Asian Americans, issues an annual report titled *Audit of Violence Against Asian Pacific*

Americans. This report is the only nongovernmental nationwide compilation and analysis of anti-Asian violence in the United States.

Although the FBI generally requires more than the utterance of a racial slur as sufficient evidence of bias motivation, NAPALC has a broader definition of hate-motivated violence, including racist language. This organization "recognizes the role of racist language in dehumanizing, humiliating, and ultimately creating an atmosphere that both fosters and condones violence against racial minorities." In its annual *Audit,* NAPALC documents hate-motivated incidents that do not result in criminal charges. This civil rights organization believes that racial slurs increase tensions, which at times escalate into physical violence.

According to the 1996 *Audit,* the number of anti-Asian incidents has increased in recent years. The report included the following retrospective statistics:

- 1996: 554 incidents
- 1995: 458 incidents
- 1994: 452 incidents
- 1993: 155 incidents (first year of the *Audit*)

NAPALC claims that racial motivation was confirmed in approximately 90 percent of the reported incidents, with the balance categorized as suspected bias cases. The type of incidents include aggravated assault, threats and intimidation, harassment, and vandalism.

A notable 1996 case was a threatening E-mail message sent to almost 60 Asian American students at the University of California at Irvine (UCI). The perpetrator, Richard Machado, stated his hatred of Asians and threatened to "personally make it [his] life career" to find and "kill" Asian students on campus. Asian Americans constitute a large percentage of the UCI student body. In the first instance of the government prosecuting a hate crime committed in cyberspace, a grand jury issued a 10-count indictment against the 19-year-old Machado, and in February 1998 a federal jury found him guilty.

It is noteworthy that the perpetrator in this case is himself Hispanic. Although hate-motivated crimes are generally assumed to be committed by whites—indeed some of the most notorious felons are white skinheads—a few of the crimes against Asian Americans involve assailants who are also members of racial minorities, as the following incidents indicate:

• Hmong refugees (an ethnic Laotian people) who had settled in a largely black west Philadelphia, Pennsylvania, neighborhood were frequently beaten and robbed by blacks during the 1980s. Some assailants reportedly believed the Hmong were receiving extra welfare benefits.

• On December 7, 1993, Colin Ferguson, a black Jamaican immigrant, murdered six people, including two Asian Americans, on the Long Island Railroad. He had previously written notes expressing hatred of Asians and whites.

• In South Central Los Angeles, California, Korean small business owners were the major targets of African American and Hispanic rioters following the verdict in the 1992 Rodney King trial. Similarly, in major cities throughout the United States—including New York, Baltimore, Chicago, and Washington, D.C.—Korean American merchants have been subjected to violent crime and racial abuse.

From a historical perspective, anti-Asian violence in the United States was much worse during the nineteenth century than it is at the present. In 1887, for instance, 31 Chinese gold miners were shot to death in Oregon. Although the current situation has improved, the increase of violent actions against Asian Americans—especially almost a dozen hate-motivated murders in the past two decades—warrants the concern of law enforcement officials and the general public.

History of Hate Crime Legislation

Although bias crimes have occurred throughout American history, it is only in the past few decades that specific legislation has been enacted in response to violent bigotry. (For the record, *bigotry* is the state of mind of a *bigot*, a person intolerantly devoted to his or her own opinions and prejudices.)

In 1981, the Anti-Defamation League (ADL), a Jewish-sponsored organization, drafted model hate crimes legislation to cover not only anti-Jewish crimes but all types of hate crimes aimed at minority groups. Currently, 41 states and the District of Columbia have enacted laws similar to or based on the ADL model. Although *expressions* of hate protected by the Bill of Rights are not criminalized, *actions* motivated by hate receive more stringent punishment. A convicted criminal is also subject to an enhanced penalty if the selected victim is chosen because of race, religion, national origin, sexual orientation, or gender. In addition, the ADL model statute includes criminal penalties for vandalism aimed at houses of worship, cemeteries, schools, and community centers. This legislation allows for victims to recover punitive damages and attorneys' fees and includes parental liability for the criminal actions of their children. In 1996, the ADL added gender to its model hate crimes legislation since these crimes are similar in nature to race- or religion-based hate crimes. Only seven states included gender in their hate crimes statutes in 1990; as of 1998, the number had grown to 20 states.

The federal government also has many civil rights statutes that cover a range of activities, including exercise of rights provided by the laws and Constitution of the United States, the exercise of religious freedom, housing-related rights, and "federally protected activities" such as voting or the right to use public accommodations. Following are descriptions of significant federal legislation on hate crimes, adapted from the ADL publication *1998 Hate Crimes Laws.*

Hate Crime Statistics Act (28 U.S. Code 534)

Enacted in 1990, this law requires the U.S. Department of Justice to acquire data from law enforcement agencies throughout the United States on crimes that "manifest prejudice based on race, religion, sexual orientation, or ethnicity" and to publish an annual summary of these findings (issued by the FBI in January). Congress expanded coverage of the law in the Violent Crime Control and Law Enforcement Act of 1994, which requires reporting on crimes based on "disability." This requirement was effective as of January 1, 1997.

According to the ADL, law enforcement agencies are gratified by this legislation. It offers them the ability to chart the national distribution of these crimes and thus discern patterns and forecast possible racial and ethnic tensions in different localities. Ideally, the act helps foster better police-community relations. Police demonstrate their concern for the welfare of citizens victimized by hate crimes in vigorously pursuing the criminal activities of violent bigots. This special reporting system also encourages victims to file charges.

Hate Crimes Sentencing Enhancement Act

A section of the Violent Crime Control and Law Enforcement Act of 1994 (Public Law 103–322), this provision requires the United States Sentencing Commission to provide a sentencing enhancement of "not less than 3 offense levels for offenses that the finders of fact at trial determine, beyond a reasonable doubt, are hate crimes." A hate crime, according to this provision, is a "crime in which the defendant intentionally selects a victim, or in the case of a property crime, the property that is the object of the crime, because of the actual or perceived race, color, religion, national origin, ethnicity, gender, disability, or sexual orientation of any person." This statute also refers to attacks and vandalism that occur in U.S. national parks or on any other federal property. The amendment took effect on November 1, 1995.

Violence Against Women Act of 1994 (42 U. S. Code 13981)

Enacted as Title IV of the Violent Crime Control and Law Enforcement Act of 1994, this act covers the increasing problem of violent crime against women. It was passed by Congress in September 1994. Under this law, "persons within the United States shall have the right to be free from crimes of violence motivated by gender." The law includes the following provisions: (1) education and training programs for police and prosecutors, (2) support for domestic violence and rape crisis centers, and (3) "a Civil Rights Remedy" for victims of gender-based violent crimes, including punitive and compensatory damage awards.

The provision for a Civil Rights Remedy, according to the ADL legal affairs department, has been challenged in recent court cases. In June 1996, a federal court judge in Connecticut upheld the constitutionality of the provision. Five other districts, however, found the law unconstitutional. As of 1999, it is expected that higher courts will rule on the constitutionality of this law in coming years.

Church Arsons Prevention Act (18 U. S. Code 247)

The series of publicized attacks against churches from 1995 through 1997 created a great deal of alarm among law enforcement agencies and the general public. Despite the widespread nature of these incidents, neither the government nor human rights organizations were able to document a national conspiracy of domestic terrorism orchestrated by violent extremists. The large number of these incidents—committed by individuals in different parts of the country acting independently—is nevertheless a worrisome phenomenon.

According to the U.S. Department of Justice, 658 investigations have been made of suspicious fires, bombings, and attempted bombings of houses of worship from January 1, 1995, to August 18, 1998. Law enforcement officials have made arrests in 225 incidents.

Sponsored by Sen. Edward Kennedy (D-MA), Sen. Lauch Faircloth (R-NC), Rep. Henry Hyde (R-IL), and Rep. John Conyers (D-MI), the Church Arsons Prevention Act was introduced to facilitate federal investigations and prosecutions of crimes against houses of worship and to amend an earlier statute enacted by Congress in 1988 mandating federal prosecution for religious vandalism incidents exceeding $10,000 in property destruction.

In an unusual bipartisan effort, both the U.S. House of Representatives and the Senate unanimously approved legislation broadening criminal prosecutions for attacks against houses of worship and establishing a loan guarantee for rebuilding. The legislation also authorized additional personnel for several agencies. The law was enacted on July 3, 1996.

As a result of the above-mentioned legislation, the executive branch of the U.S. government has been involved in the following initiatives and ongoing activities (this information was adapted from the ADL publications *1998 Hate Crimes Laws* and *1999 Hate Crimes Laws*):

• As of September 1998, the FBI had held more than 126 hate-crime training conferences across the United States for nearly 7,700 law enforcement officials from more than 2,600 agencies.

• The Community Relations Service, the only U.S. government agency primarily mandated to assist localities in dealing with intergroup conflicts, has served an important role in the implementation of the Hate Crime Statistics Act by training police and law enforcement officials.

• In 1992, the Office for Victims of Crime in the U.S. Department of Justice provided a grant for developing a training curriculum to improve the response of professionals to victims of hate crimes.

• In 1993, the Office of Juvenile Justice and Delinquency Prevention provided $100,000 for a study to identify the characteristics and types of juveniles who commit hate crimes (*Report to Congress on Juvenile Hate Crime*, July 1996). This branch of the U.S. Justice Department also provided funding for a "Healing the Hate" curriculum to assist the prevention and treatment of hate crimes committed by young people.

• Under funding provided by the Bureau of Justice Assistance (BJA), the National Criminal Justice Association issued a "Policymaker's Guide to Hate Crimes," which included a survey of legal cases and law enforcement hate crime practices.

• In July 1996, the U.S. Department of Education provided almost $2 million in grants to develop "innovative, effective strategies for preventing and reducing the incidence of crimes and conflicts motivated by hate in localities directly affected by hate crimes."

• Also that month, the U.S. Commission on Civil Rights held hearings on the arson attacks directed at houses of worship in six southern states.

• The Anti-Defamation League and other human rights organizations and professionals have assisted in a model hate-crime training curriculum for use by the federal Law Enforcement Training Centers, a program of the U.S. Department of Treasury.

• The Department of Housing and Urban Development has organized seminars to discuss a $10 million loan guarantee rebuilding fund for houses of worship devastated in hate-motivated arson attacks. Under the National Rebuilding Initiative Program of HUD, more than 100 institutions will receive assistance.

U.S. Supreme Court Decisions

Although most legislation on hate crimes was enacted during the early and mid-1990s, numerous court cases have challenged the constitutional and legal grounds of these statutes. Two of the most important cases were eventually argued in the U.S. Supreme Court.

The first case involved a group of white skinheads who burned a cross in the yard of a black family in St. Paul, Minnesota, on June 21, 1990. Soon after, 17-year-old Robert A. Viktora was charged and later convicted of violating the local "bias-motivated crime" ordinance, which banned the burning cross and Nazi swastika. The statute stipulated that these symbols "arouse anger, alarm, or resentment in others on the basis of race, color, creed, religion or gender." Appealing the conviction to a Minnesota district court, the lawyer for Viktora claimed the law violated his First Amendment right of free speech. The district court ruled in favor of the defendant, overturning the conviction and declaring the law unconstitutional. The court claimed that the St. Paul ordinance was too broad in its application and violated First Amendment rights of freedom of expression.

In a counter appeal brought by the City of St. Paul, the Minnesota Supreme Court ruled that the local ordinance was valid because cross burning was similar to "fighting words"—a phrase used in a 1942 landmark U.S. Supreme Court decision—that incited violence and hence was not protected by the First Amendment of the Constitution.

R. A. V. v. City of St. Paul was finally brought before the U.S. Supreme Court on June 22, 1992. In a unanimous decision, the justices agreed that the St. Paul ordinance violated the First Amendment. Although offering separate legal arguments, the justices struck down the ordinance because it was unconstitutionally broad: the law had not criminalized all fighting words but only certain words based on their content or viewpoint and thus violated the First Amendment. The decision declared that pure or symbolic bias-motivated speech, no matter how damaging to the intended target, cannot be outlawed solely on the basis of its effect on the victim.

A subsequent decision of the U.S. Supreme Court, however, did establish the legality of other types of hate crime legislation. The *Wisconsin v. Mitchell* case began on October 7, 1989, when a group of young black men and boys gathered at an apartment complex in Kenosha, Wisconsin. After discussing a scene from the motion picture *Mississippi Burning* in which a white man beat a young black person, the group went outside and saw a young white boy on the opposite side of the street. Todd Mitchell, a 19-year-old African American, then shouted, "There goes a white boy, go get him." The group ran toward the boy and severely beat him. He was rendered unconscious and remained in a coma for four days.

After a jury trial in the Kenosha Circuit Court, Mitchell was convicted of aggravated battery. Although the offense generally carries a maximum sentence of two years imprisonment, the jury found that the defendant intentionally selected his victim because of the boy's race and increased his sentence to seven years based on the Wisconsin hate penalty enhancement statute. (The Wisconsin statute, modeled after the Anti-Defamation League's proposed hate-crime law, mandates increased penalties for a crime when the victim is targeted because of "race, religion, color, disability, sexual orientation, national origin or ancestry of that person.")

Mitchell's attorney claimed that the additional punishment violated his right to free speech, and the Wisconsin Supreme Court concurred by reversing the judgment. The Court held that the penalty enhancement statute "violates the First Amendment directly by punishing what the legislature has deemed to be offensive thought." The decision also stated that "the Wisconsin legislature cannot criminalize bigoted thought with which it disagrees."

The State of Wisconsin appealed the decision of the Wisconsin Supreme Court. On June 11, 1993, the U.S. Supreme Court in *Wisconsin v. Mitchell* reversed the Wisconsin Court ruling. In a unanimous decision, the justices agreed that the hate penalty enhancement ordinance does not violate the First Amendment. The Court held that the enhanced penalty is appropriate "because this conduct is thought to inflict greater individual and societal harm." Furthermore, the justices argued that the statute would not stifle free speech because the bias motivation would have to be connected with a specific act; the law focused on a person's actions, not on an individual's bigoted ideas.

The Anti-Defamation League, among other human rights organizations, promptly praised the U.S. Supreme Court decision. "Hate crime laws are necessary because the failure to recognize and effectively address this type of crime can cause an isolated incident to fester and explode into widespread community tensions," asserts an ADL publication.

Hate Crime Legislation at the State Level

Following this landmark Supreme Court decision, numerous states have upheld local and municipal penalty enhancement statutes for bias-motivated crimes. According to the ADL publication *1998 Hate Crimes Laws*, four state courts—Ohio, Oregon, Washington, and Wisconsin—have recently upheld the constitutionality of these laws.

The actions of these states are especially significant because most prosecutions of bias-motivated violence occur at the state level. Many state legislatures have expressed similar concerns to the State of Washington government, which enacted the following statement:

> The legislature finds that crimes and threats against persons because of their race, color, religion, ancestry, national origin, gender, sexual orientation or mental, physical or sensory handicaps are serious and increasing. The legislature also finds that crimes and threats are often directed against interracial couples and their children or couples of mixed religions, colors, ancestries or national origins because of bias and bigotry. . . . The legislature finds that protection of those citizens from threats of harm due to bias and bigotry is a compelling state interest. (*Washington Rev. Code Ann.*)

Almost all states currently have some type of law that criminalizes hate or bias-motivated crime. These statutes cover the following:

• Institutional violence—prohibiting the defacing or vandalizing of synagogues, churches, schools, cemeteries, monuments, and community centers.

• Bias-motivated violence and intimidation—these statutes prosecute individuals for intimidating, harassing, trespassing upon the property of, or assaulting an individual because of the person's religion, race, gender, nationality, or sexual orientation.

• Prohibition of particular acts that have traditionally been associated with racial hatred, such as cross burning or mask or hood wearing. In 1951, for example, the State of Georgia passed an antimask law because of the violence and intimidation carried out by mask-wearing members of the Ku Klux Klan. (These laws, however, exempt holiday costume masks or other "innocent activities.")

• A large number of states have enacted statutes that provide compensation to the victims of hate crimes. These laws specify monetary damages (including damages for emotional distress and punitive damages), attorney fees, and other costs of litigation.

• Some states require law enforcement officials to receive special training on identifying and dealing with cases of hate crime. In addition, some states, such as California, have enacted special sentencing for hate crime perpetrators—as a condition of probation—to attend programs on racial or ethnic sensitivity.

• Some state legislatures have provided school districts with funding to implement programs designed to reduce and prevent hate-motivated incidents.

• Finally, several states require law enforcement agencies to maintain statistics on reported incidents of hate crimes. Reporting hate crime data, according to experts, may enhance public awareness of the growing problem.

Almost all state laws, similar to federal legislation, include race, color, religion, and national origin among the protected characteristics. Some state laws also protect sex or gender, disability, and sexual orientation.

A few statutes include other protected characteristics such as age (District of Columbia, Iowa, Minnesota, and Vermont), political affiliation (Iowa, West Virginia), and involvement in human rights activities (Montana). The District of Columbia law covers the widest range of categories, including prejudice based on "actual or perceived race, color, religion, national origin, sex, age, marital status, personal appearance, sexual orientation, family responsibility, physical handicap, matriculation or political affiliation."

Critics of Hate Crime Laws

In the past few years, several legal scholars, including James B. Jacobs, a New York University law professor, and Susan Gellman, assistant public defender for the Ohio Public Defender Commission, have written eloquent essays in various law and academic journals raising serious legal, constitutional, and political questions about the need for hate crime legislation.

Writing in the *UCLA Law Review,* Gellman summarized the basic stance of many critics:

Those who oppose ethnic intimidation laws, or at least who question them most vigorously, do not disagree that bigotry (and certainly bigotry-related crime) is a serious problem. On the contrary, they are also from the ranks of the most civil rights-conscious thinkers and activists. These critics focus on threats to constitutional liberties under the First and Fourteenth Amendments.

Their concerns are that these laws tread dangerously close to criminalization of speech and thought, that they impermissibly distinguish among people based on their beliefs, and that they are frequently too vaguely drafted to provide adequate notice of prohibited conduct. In addition, these critics question the wisdom of enacting such laws; even if they can be drafted in a way that does not offend the Constitution, they may ultimately undercut their own goals more than they serve them.

Jacobs and coauthor Kimberly A. Potter, writing in volume 22 of *Crime and Justice: A Review of Research,* raise questions about the sociological and criminological consequences of hate crime legislation:

The concept of hate crime is easy to grasp as an ideal type, but it is difficult to effectuate in a workaday criminal justice system. Most putative hate crimes are not ideologically motivated murders, although some of those do occur. . . . Whether it aids understanding of their conduct and of our society to brand them as bigots as well as criminals is not an easy question to answer.

Beyond the problem of definition, labeling particular incidents as hate crimes bristles with subjectivity and potential for bias. Nevertheless, the very existence of the term, the attempt to measure the incidence of hate crime, and the prosecution and sentencing of some offenders under different types of hate crime statutes have already changed how Americans think about the crime problem. At a minimum, the new hate crime laws have contributed further to politicizing the crime problem.

. . . Rather than Americans pulling together and affirming their common ground by condemning criminal conduct, they may now increasingly see crime as a polarizing issue that pits one social group against another, thereby further dividing an already fractured society.

Conclusions

Few proponents of hate crime legislation believe that these statutes will eradicate the growing problem of hate-motivated violence in the United States. The festering problem of racism, anti-

Semitism, and other forms of bigotry offers no easy legal solution. However, hate crime laws and sentencing have certainly helped many victims and presumably aided the safety and welfare of numerous communities. When a judge requires a youth involved in an anti-Jewish crime to serve time in prison, or the inciters of skinhead violence against African Americans are forced to pay restitution to the families of victims, or antigay felons are fully prosecuted for their crimes, violent bigots and their ilk are made aware that their hate-motivated criminal actions will have punitive consequences. This type of legislation is only about a decade old, and it is still too soon to assess its full impact or success. Nevertheless, many human rights professionals agree that it is a useful interim measure in the long-term battle against hate crimes.

Chronology 2

Because the number of individual violent hate crimes committed in the United States during the past few decades is too large for a comprehensive list, the following chronology is necessarily selective. The list has been compiled to demonstrate the wide range of these crimes and to illustrate why some groups are calling for legislation to deter and prevent their future occurrence. The chronology also contains notable events in the legislative and judicial history of hate crimes laws. Much of the information regarding crimes committed before 1979 has been adapted from the outstanding reference work *Racial and Religious Violence in the United States: A Chronology* (New York: Garland, 1991) by Michael and Judy Ann Newton.

The chronology begins in 1955, the year Emmett Till was lynched in Mississippi, an event many historians consider the beginning of the modern civil rights movement. (For further information, see Stephen J. Whitfield, *A Death in the Delta: The Story of Emmett Till,* New York: Free Press, 1988.)

1955   May 7. Rev. George W. Lee, an official of the National Association for the Advancement of Colored People (NAACP), is shot and killed on a highway in Belzoni, Mississippi.

1955
cont.

August 13. Lamar Smith, a vocal supporter for black voter registration, is shot and killed on the lawn of the county courthouse in Brookhaven, Mississippi.

August 28. Emmett Till, a 14-year-old black boy, is kidnapped, shot, and drowned in a river near Money, Mississippi, for allegedly whistling at a white man's wife. His killers are acquitted after a controversial trial. This notorious incident is often considered the catalyst for the modern civil rights movement.

October 22. John Reese, a 16-year-old African American, is killed and two other black youths are wounded by white gunmen at a local cafe in Mayflower, Texas. The attack is one of several violent incidents aimed at discouraging the black community from building a new school.

1956

January 30. A bomb explodes at the Montgomery, Alabama, home of the Reverend Martin Luther King Jr.

February 3–4. The admission of Autherine Lucy, a black coed, to the University of Alabama sparks a riot from local Klansmen and white students. Another riot occurs on February 6, which leads university administrators to suspend and later expel Lucy from the university.

April 11. Six Ku Klux Klan members assault singer Nat "King" Cole during a performance at the Birmingham, Alabama, municipal auditorium.

1957

January 23. Willie Edwards, a black truck driver, is abducted by Klansmen in Montgomery, Alabama. He is accused of attacking white women and forced at gunpoint to leap from a river bridge. His body is later recovered, and his death, considered accidental until 1976, is charged as a homicide when a Klansman confesses. Three other Klansmen are indicted, but the charges are dismissed when the prosecution fails to prove the cause of Edwards's death was drowning. In 1998, Montgomery District Attorney Ellen Brooks ordered an exhumation and the coroner found the death was indeed caused by drowning.

1958   March 16. The Jewish Community Center in Nashville, Tennessee, is dynamited.

August 24–25. Two formerly all-white schools in Deep Creek, North Carolina, are destroyed by fire after they were scheduled to be integrated.

June 29. A black miner removes a package of dynamite from a Baptist church in Birmingham, Alabama, whose pastor is civil rights leader Rev. F. L. Shuttlesworth. The dynamite explodes in the street, breaking windows in a four-block area.

July 7. An early morning explosion damages the home of the Reverend Warren Carr, the white chairman of the Durham, North Carolina, Human Relations Committee, a local group devoted to improving racial relationships.

October 12. The Temple, an Atlanta synagogue, is bombed at 3:30 A.M., causing an estimated $200,000 in damage. The blast tears an 18-square-foot hole in a side entrance of the building and shatters windows of a nearby building and apartment house. Twenty minutes after the blast, a caller says it was the "last empty building I'll blow up in Atlanta." The bombings and phone calls parallel synagogue attacks in Miami, Jacksonville, and Birmingham during this time.

1959   April 25. Mack Parker, a black truck driver, is taken from his jail cell, where he was being held for suspected rape, and is lynched by a mob of whites in Poplarville, Mississippi. An area prosecutor refuses to accept FBI evidence naming several of the lynchers. When the state trooper who arrested Parker offers his gun to the husband of the rape victim so that he can shoot Parker, the husband refuses because his wife's description of the perpetrator is unclear.

1960   January 7–8. Teenage vandals are arrested in a wave of anti-Jewish vandalism at synagogues and other buildings in New York City, Philadelphia, Chicago, Boston, and more than a dozen other cities.

1960
cont.
April 23. William Moore, a northern white civil rights advocate, is shot and killed in Attalla, Alabama, during a one-man civil rights march from Tennessee to Mississippi. On April 27, a local white man is charged with the murder.

1961
September 25. Herbert Lee, a cotton farmer and black voter registration organizer, is shot to death by E. H. Hurst in the town of Liberty, Mississippi. Hurst, a white neighbor and state legislator, is never brought to trial.

1962
April 9. Roman Ducksworth, a black soldier, is shot to death by a white policeman for refusing to sit in the back of a bus in Taylorsville, Mississippi.

1963
June 8. The county sheriff and police chief of Winona, Mississippi, and three other whites are indicted on federal charges of brutalizing black prisoners.

June 12. Medgar Evers, a black NAACP leader, is killed by a sniper in the driveway of his home in Jackson, Mississippi. The Federal Bureau of Investigation finds the murderer is Byron de la Beckwith, a member of the KKK and White Citizens' Council. However, two murder trials result in hung juries. In 1967, Beckwith runs for Mississippi governor with the backing of the Ku Klux Klan. After prosecutors tried Beckwith a third time, he was convicted on February 5, 1994, and sentenced to life imprisonment at the Central Mississippi Correctional Facility.

September 4. The Birmingham, Alabama, home of Arthur Shores, a black attorney, is bombed for a second time, touching off a riot resulting in one death and eighteen injuries. On the same day, 125 members of the National States Rights Party, a neo-Nazi racist organization, scuffle with police outside a recently integrated school.

September 15. A bomb explodes at the 16th Street Baptist Church in Birmingham, Alabama, during Sunday services. Four black girls are killed: Addie Mae Collins, Cynthia Wesley, Carole Robertson, and Denise McNair.

Another person is blinded. In reaction, African Americans riot. Alabama state troopers under the command of Al Lingo, a "good friend" of the Ku Klux Klan, try to disperse the rioters. During the outbreak, a policeman "accidentally" kills Johnny Robinson, a black youth. Virgil Ware, a 13-year-old, is also fatally shot by two white youths.

1964   January 31. Louis Allen, a witness to the 1961 murder of Herbert Lee, is shot and killed in the front yard of his home in Liberty, Mississippi.

April 7. Rev. Bruce Klunder, a white minister from Cleveland, Ohio, is crushed to death by a bulldozer while protesting the construction of a segregated school.

May 2. Henry Dee and Charlie Moore, two African American teenagers, are abducted by Klansmen in Meadville, Mississippi. Two months later, their bodies are pulled from a nearby river. Although murder charges are filed against two KKK members, they are later dismissed.

June 10. A white mob hurling bricks and sulfuric acid breaks through police lines to attack black demonstrators in St. Augustine, Florida. Police use tear gas to disperse the rioters.

June 21. In Philadelphia, Mississippi, civil rights workers Michael Schwerner, James Chaney, and Andrew Goodman are arrested for allegedly speeding. They are released to a waiting gang of Ku Klux Klansmen who murder them on a rural road and later bury them in an earthen dam. On August 4, their bodies are recovered. Although the State of Mississippi refuses to file murder charges, the seven Klansmen are later convicted of federal civil rights violations.

June 25. A black church in Longdale, Mississippi, is damaged by a firebomb.

June 26. Arsonists burn a black church in Clinton, Mississippi.

1964
cont.

July 6. Two black churches in Raleigh, Mississippi, are burned to the ground.

July 10. Three rabbis active in black voter registration programs in Hattiesburg, Mississippi, are assaulted with metal clubs. On August 8, two white men plead guilty to the attacks, pay $500 fines, and receive 90-day suspended sentences.

July 11. Ku Klux Klansmen in Colbert, Georgia, ambush a carload of black army reserve officers returning home from summer training exercises. Lt. Col. Lemuel Penn is killed by shotgun blasts; his companions escape unharmed. Two Klan members are acquitted of murder charges, but both are later sentenced to prison for federal civil rights violations.

1965

February 10. Deputies armed with electric prods force civil rights marchers out of Selma, Alabama, leaving them stranded more than a mile from town.

February 17. A voter registration headquarters is set on fire by KKK members in Laurel, Mississippi.

February 18. Jimmy Lee Jackson, a black civil rights worker, is beaten and fatally shot in Marion, Alabama, when state law enforcement officers attack about 400 black demonstrators. While Jackson lies in a Selma, Alabama, hospital, police serve him an arrest warrant. He dies on February 26.
   In Bessemer, Alabama, Klansmen refuse to work with black employees at the W. S. Dickey Clay Company. They shoot at the car of a nonstriking worker and damage the plant.

March 9. In Selma, Alabama, violent racists attack Rev. James Reeb, a Boston minister active in the civil rights movement. He is fatally beaten. The defendants are acquitted by a jury that earlier discussed their verdict with Sheriff Jim Clark, an avowed racist.

March 21. A desegregated cafe is firebombed in Vicksburg, Mississippi.

March 25. Viola Liuzzo, a white civil rights worker, is ambushed and killed by KKK members in Lowndesboro, Alabama.

March 29. Members of the Klan hurl a tear gas grenade at blacks in Bogalusa, Louisiana.

May 13. An African American church in Oxford, Alabama, is wrecked by a bomb.

May 17. A gas station and a motel owned by vocal Klan opponents are bombed in Laurel, Mississippi.

June 2. Oneal Moore and Creed Rogers, two black sheriff deputies, are ambushed while on patrol in Bogalusa, Louisiana; Rogers is wounded, and Moore is fatally injured. On June 5, gunshots are fired at the home of the law enforcement official investigating the murder. Although Ray McElveen, a KKK member, is charged with the death, he is not prosecuted. As of 1998, the New Orleans office of the Anti-Defamation League is trying to reopen the case.

June 16. KKK members shoot at a black-owned nightclub and also at the state vice president of the NAACP in separate incidents in Laurel, Mississippi.

July 1. In Laurel, Mississippi, Klansmen burn a civil rights organization headquarters and thirteen homes occupied by civil rights workers.

July 15. Willie Brewster, a black man, is shot and killed in Anniston, Alabama, by nightriders following a rally organized by the National States Rights Party.

July 16. While police stand and watch, white mobs attack black protesters in Bogalusa, Louisiana. After the seventh assault, police arrest two white attackers. On July 17, whites spray water hoses on black demonstrators and hurl rocks and bottles.

In Greensboro, Alabama, about 75 black demonstrators are attacked by a white mob armed with clubs, hammers, and rubber hoses. Seventeen demonstrators require hospitalization.

1965
cont.

July 18. An African American church in Elmwood, Alabama, is burned. Arsonists burn two black churches in Greensboro, Alabama. The Imperial Wizard of the Ku Klux Klan, Sam Bowers, claims that the Klan is responsible for more than 16 arson fires in Laurel, Mississippi.

July 27. Two black homes are firebombed in Ferriday, Louisiana. The office of the Congress of Racial Equality (CORE) is firebombed in New Orleans, Louisiana.

July 31. The headquarters of the Council of Federated Organizations in Columbia, Mississippi, is damaged by fire and subjected to gunfire in a predawn attack.

August 20. Jonathan Daniels, a white seminary student on leave from the Episcopal Theological School in Cambridge, Massachusetts, is shot and killed by a part-time deputy sheriff and a KKK member in Hayneville, Alabama. Robert F. Morrisoe, a Catholic priest from Chicago, is also seriously wounded in the same attack.

August 23. Rev. Donald A. Thompson, a Unitarian minister who is involved in civil rights work in Jackson, Mississippi, is seriously wounded in an ambush.

August 26. At a rally in Plymouth, North Carolina, Klansmen beat 27 black protesters.

August 27. George Metcalfe, an NAACP official, is maimed when a bomb explodes in his car in Natchez, Mississippi. Although FBI agents find Klan members responsible, no prosecutions result.

September 26. A black church in Jones County, Mississippi, is burned by arsonists.

October 4. In Crawfordsville, Georgia, the Grand Dragon of the KKK assaults a black demonstrator.

November 18. Gunshots are fired at four civil rights workers in Victoria, Virginia, injuring one person.

November 29. Three persons are injured from a car bomb

planted near a black-owned grocery store in Vicksburg, Mississippi, close to the site of a local civil rights meeting.

December 15. Lee Culbreath, a black newspaper boy, is shot and killed by two white men in Hamburg, Arkansas. Police charge two Ku Klux Klan members with the murder.

December 31. A store owned by John Nosser—the mayor of Natchez, Mississippi, and a vocal opponent of the Klan—is destroyed by arson.

1966   January 2. An African American church in Newton, Georgia, is burned. Anonymous callers threaten the life of the local sheriff if he investigates the incident.

January 3. Samuel Younge Jr., a black college student, is shot and killed in Tuskeegee, Alabama, for trying to use a "whites only" restroom.

January 10. After volunteering to pay the poll taxes for black voters, civil rights activist Vernon Dahmer is fatally burned in a firebomb attack in his Hattiesburg, Mississippi, home. Samuel Bowers, an Imperial Wizard of the KKK, was tried four times for the murder, resulting in deadlocked juries. On August 21, 1998, a multiracial jury convicted him of murder and arson.

January 30. The Atlanta-based Southern Regional Council issues a report stating that southern whites had killed a total of 14 local blacks and civil rights workers in 1965 and three blacks thus far in 1966.

February 19. A "bomb factory" created by Birmingham, Alabama, whites is found in the woods outside of town.

February 24. A recently integrated high school in Elba, Alabama, is damaged by two dynamite blasts.

April 2. Bombs explode at two swimming pools in Baton Rouge, Louisiana, that were scheduled to be integrated facilities.

1966
cont.

April 9. Bombs destroy a black church in Ernul, North Carolina.

June 6. Civil rights worker James Meredith is wounded by three gunshots during a one-person "march against fear" in Hernando, Mississippi. The hospital treating Meredith receives threats from a caller describing himself as a KKK member.

June 10. Ben White, an elderly black man, is kidnapped and shot to death in Natchez, Mississippi, by Klansmen who believe the murder will attract the Reverend Martin Luther King Jr. to the area. The Klansmen are acquitted of murder charges on December 9, 1967. White's relatives file a civil suit for wrongful death and win more than $1 million in damages on November 13, 1968. The defendant, Ernest Avants, avoided paying any money by placing his assets in his first wife's name.

June 17. News reporters covering a civil rights rally in Greenwood, Mississippi, escape injury after two poisonous snakes are tossed into their vehicle.

June 21. Civil rights marchers are assaulted by white mobs in Philadelphia, Mississippi, while police stand by, watching.

June 24. A mob of whites pelt the Reverend Martin Luther King Jr. and other demonstrators with eggs and missiles in Philadelphia, Mississippi. Arsonists destroy a Catholic church in Carthage, Mississippi.

July 1. Klansmen bomb a store in Milwaukee, Wisconsin, owned by the former president of the Wisconsin Civil Rights Congress.

July 3. Klansmen pelt police with stones in Lebanon, Ohio, after two KKK members are arrested for violating the state's antimask law.

July 10. Two whites are arrested after firing a submachine gun at a federal officer and two civil rights workers outside an African American church in Grenada, Mississippi.

July 18. Jeering whites assault civil rights marchers in Jacksonville, Florida.

July 20. A black-owned store in Jacksonville, Florida, is firebombed.

July 28. Following a rally of the white racist National States Rights Party, white gangs invade a black neighborhood in Baltimore, Maryland. Three members are charged with inciting a riot and are sentenced to a two-year prison term.

July 30. Charles Triggs, a black bricklayer, is shot and killed by two white gunmen in Bogalusa, Louisiana.

July 31. White mobs stone a civil rights procession led by the Reverend Martin Luther King Jr. in Chicago. Fifty-four persons are injured, including two police officers.

September 12–13. A mob of almost 400 whites riot in Grenada, Mississippi, in opposition to school integration. Police stand by while blacks and news reporters are beaten with ax handles, chains, and steel pipes. Two black youths are hospitalized with serious injuries.

September 24. Arsonists destroy the Cleveland, Ohio, home of Rev. John Compton, a black minister.

October 5. A black church in Richmond, Virginia, is bombed.

November 8. Violent incidents against blacks participating in local elections occur in Lowndes County, Alabama, and in Amite County, Mississippi.

November 20. James Motley, a black man, is beaten to death in a jail cell in Wetumpka, Alabama. A jury acquits Sheriff Harvey Conner of murder on April 12, 1967.

1967   January 10. Vandals desecrate more than 100 graves at two Jewish cemeteries in New Orleans, Louisiana.

April 25. Bombs damage the home of the mother of

1967
cont. Judge Frank Johnson in Birmingham, Alabama. Judge Johnson, a vocal opponent of the Klan, had issued several decisions in support of school integration.

May 14. A black-owned home in a predominantly white suburb of Cleveland, Ohio, is bombed.

July 18. FBI agents arrest 12 whites, including at least 7 Klansmen, for violent racist acts committed over a 21-month period in Rowan and Cabarrus Counties, North Carolina. In a separate incident in Greensboro, North Carolina, two Klansmen are jailed for a cross-burning.

August 28. White mobs shouting "We want slaves!" and "Get yourself a nigger!" stone NAACP demonstrators in Milwaukee, Mississippi. Marchers are again attacked the next day while the Freedom House is destroyed by arsonists.

September 18. Temple Beth Israel in Jackson, Mississippi, is bombed. As FBI agents pursue suspects, their vehicle is rammed from the rear by a carload of armed KKK members.

October 6. Snipers fire into the home of an NAACP worker in Carthage, Mississippi.

November 21. The home of Rabbi Perry Nussbaum in Jackson, Mississippi, is bombed. Nussbaum and his wife, Arene, narrowly escape death.

1968 February 8. Three black students, Henry E. Smith, Delano H. Middleton, and Samuel Hammond Jr., are killed, and at least 34 others are wounded when state police fire on rioters at South Carolina State College in Orangeburg. Campus unrest began when college demonstrators started picketing a segregated local bowling alley.

April 4. Rev. Martin Luther King Jr. is assassinated by a sniper on the eve of a scheduled protest demonstration in Memphis, Tennessee. Nationwide rioting erupts in more than 125 cities over the next week, leaving 46 persons dead, 2,600 injured, and 21,270 arrested. Damage from arson and vandalism is estimated at $45 million.

August 14. The church of Rev. A. D. King is bombed in Louisville, Kentucky.

August 16–17. Two white men murder the black female proprietor of a tavern in Cincinnati, Ohio. A riot erupts, and one black youth is critically shot while stoning police cars.

November 25. A Bronx, New York, Hebrew school is damaged in a suspicious fire. It is the tenth attack on Jewish institutions in New York City in the past three months.

November 27. The Yeshiva of Eastern Parkway in Brooklyn, New York, is destroyed in a fire. On November 29, two teenagers are charged with arson.

December 24. Gunshots are fired into the home of a black Office of Economic Opportunity administrator in Monroe, Louisiana. Although a Klansman is arrested, he is set free in February 1969.

1970   January 19. Fire damages a Bronx, New York, synagogue that was vandalized four times in the past year.

January 28. Vandals paint swastikas and light a fire at the Intervale Jewish Center in the Bronx.

March 3. A mob of whites attack school buses carrying black students to recently integrated schools in Lamar, South Carolina. Three rioters are convicted on February 17, 1971.

August 30. Ten buses scheduled for use in desegregating schools in Pontiac, Michigan, are bombed. Six members of the Ku Klux Klan are arrested, including Robert Miles, a major national neo-Nazi leader.

September 10. A bomb with more than a dozen sticks of dynamite is found under a Jacksonville, Florida, school bus and defused.

1973   September 16. KKK member Byron de la Beckwith is arrested; firearms and a time bomb are found in his automobile. Beckwith was planning a raid on the home of a local Jewish leader. The Louisiana Klan conducts a fundraising campaign for Beckwith's legal defense, and he is acquitted of all charges on January 16, 1974.

October 2. Evelyn Walker, a white woman, is doused with gasoline and burned to death by black youths after her car breaks down in a black neighborhood in Boston, Massachusetts.

October 6. Kirk Miller, a white cab driver, is the victim of a racially motivated murder in Boston.

October 19. Members of the San Francisco, California, based Black Muslim splinter group the Death Angels, assault white victims Richard and Quita Hague with machetes, killing the woman and leaving her husband severely injured. Members of this violent group reportedly earn their "angel wings" by killing white men and women. The killings begin in October and continue for about six months, resulting in the deaths of 14 men and women and leaving 7 wounded. The case was nicknamed "Zebra" because a special police task force used the last radio frequency, Z, for communication.

October 29. Frances Rose, a white woman, is shot dead in another Zebra killing in San Francisco, California. Jessie Cooks, arrested near the scene, is sentenced to life in prison for the murder.

November 21. The Sephardic Institute for Advanced Learning in New York City is damaged and one employee is killed during an arson attack. A second fire on November 23 destroys the institute.

November 26. Rev. Edward Pace, a black minister in Gadsden, Alabama, is shot and killed in his home. A KKK member is convicted of the murder on March 9, 1974.

1974   January 28. Death Angel gunmen kill Tana White and

Jane Holly in random, racially motivated attacks in the San Francisco, California, area.

April 14. Ward Anderson and Terry White are shot by Death Angel gunmen at a San Francisco bus stop.

April 19. Frank Carlson, a white grocer, is murdered and his wife is beaten and raped by an African American who claims to be one of the Zebra killers. Police arrest seven Death Angel suspects on May 1; four are convicted and sentenced to life in prison.

July 27. Shootings are reported during a local Ku Klux Klan recruiting drive in Kokomo, Indiana.

August 16. Judge Arthur Gamble, who signed the murder indictments against three Klan members involved in the murder of Viola Liuzzo in 1965, is injured by a car bomb in Greenville, Alabama.

September 19. Dr. Charles Glatt, who worked for the city of Dayton, Ohio, to prepare school desegregation plans, is shot and killed at work. Police arrest Neal Long, who had been linked to a series of racist murders that killed six local blacks and wounded more than a dozen others in the 1970s.

November 11. In the Boro Park section of Brooklyn, New York, two synagogues, a Jewish school, and the homes of two Hasidic Jews are firebombed.

1976   February 26. Four members of the Ku Klux Klan are indicted for the murder of Willie Edwards in Montgomery, Alabama, in 1957. Charges are later dismissed.

April 6. In Boston, Massachusetts, Theodore Landsmark, a black attorney, is attacked by a white youth who attempted to stab him with an American flagpole. The Pulitzer Prize–winning news photograph of this incident is published in newspapers around the world.

September 8. White youths shouting racial epithets randomly attack blacks and Hispanics in Washington

1976
cont.
Square Park in Greenwich Village, New York. Marcus Mota is killed, and several others are injured. Five youths are sentenced to prison terms ranging from 3 to 25 years.

1977
February 14. Fred Cowan, a self-styled neo-Nazi who was a member of the racist National States Rights Party, kills five persons and wounds five others before committing suicide in New Rochelle, New York. He was previously suspended from work after a conflict with a Jewish supervisor.

April 15–17. In a series of violent incidents in Elwood, Indiana, Klan members burn crosses and scatter garbage on the lawns of local residents. The mayor's home is also targeted with shotgun pellets.

1978
August 7. Alphonse Manning and Toni Schwenn, an interracial couple, are killed by racist murderer Joseph Paul Franklin in Madison, Wisconsin.

September 5. A white youth wearing a Nazi armband fires on black picnickers in Jonesville, North Carolina, killing one man and wounding three. A second victim dies on September 7. The gunman commits suicide.

October 8. A sniper, later believed to be neo-Nazi murderer Joseph Paul Franklin, kills Gerald Gordon while he is leaving a bar mitzvah in Richmond Heights, a suburb of St. Louis, Missouri.

November 18. Former Ku Klux Klan member Robert Chambliss is convicted of murder in the bombing of the 16th Street Baptist Church in Birmingham, Alabama, on September 15, 1963, which killed four black girls.
Four African American churches in Wilkes County, Georgia, are burned by arsonists. A white man who confessed to the crime is sentenced to six years in prison.

1979
The Anti-Defamation League (ADL) issues its first *Audit of Anti-Semitic Incidents*.

October 21. Jessie Taylor and Marion Bresette, an interracial couple, are shot and killed in a parking lot in Oklahoma City. Joseph Paul Franklin is later charged in the case, but the indictments are dismissed in 1983.

1980   January 8. Joseph Paul Franklin kills Larry E. Reese, an African American man, at a local fast-food restaurant in Indianapolis, Indiana.

August 19. Joseph Paul Franklin, a former member of the Ku Klux Klan and American Nazi Party, murders David Martin and Theodore Fields, two black men who jogged alongside two white women in a park in Salt Lake City, Utah. Franklin was later connected to other crimes including the bombing of Beth Shalom synagogue in Chattanooga on July 29, 1977; the shooting of former National Urban League director Vernon Jordan on May 29, 1980; the murders of Darrell Lane and Dante Evans Brown in a vacant Cincinnati lot on June 6, 1980; and the murders of Kathleen Mikula and Arthur Smothers in Johnstown, Pennsylvania, on June 15, 1980. Franklin was involved in the slaying of 21 people who were either interracial couples or Jews.

1981   The Anti-Defamation League drafts the first Model Hate Crimes legislation.

1982   June 19. Vincent Chin, a young Chinese American, was brutally murdered in Detroit by unemployed autoworkers who apparently believed him to be Japanese. The case received national attention when the judge placed the assailants on probation and required them to pay a $3,000 fine each.

1984   The National Gay and Lesbian Task Force issues its first report on antigay violence in the United States.

June 18. Alan Berg, a popular Denver, Colorado, radio talk show host, is murdered in a machine-gun attack in the driveway of his home. His assailants are members of a neo-Nazi group.

1985   March 21. The U.S. House of Representatives Committee on the Judiciary holds its first congressional hearing to discuss the passage of a law to require the U.S. Justice

1985   Department to collect and publish statistics on hate
cont.   crimes.

          December 24. Charles Goldmark, a Seattle, Washington,
          attorney, is brutally murdered by a drifter named David
          Lewis Rice, who had close ties with racist and anti-Jew-
          ish groups. Rice thought that Goldmark, a prominent lib-
          eral lawyer, "looked Jewish."

1986   July 16. The U.S. House of Representatives Committee
          on the Judiciary holds hearings to examine reports
          of harassment and violence directed against Arab
          Americans.

          October 9. The U.S. House of Representatives Committee
          on the Judiciary holds hearings to examine the problem
          of violence against gay men and lesbians.

          December 20. A gang of white teenagers in the Howard
          Beach section of Queens, New York, attack Michael Grif-
          fith, an African American who was passing through their
          neighborhood. They beat and chase him to his death on
          a nearby highway. His stepfather, Cedric Sandiford, is se-
          verely beaten.

1987   November 10. The U.S. House of Representatives Com-
          mittee on the Judiciary holds hearings on the causes of
          and possible responses to recent violent acts committed
          against Asians and Asian Americans.

1988   May 11–July 12. The U.S. House of Representatives Com-
          mittee on the Judiciary holds hearings to consider legis-
          lation to establish a Commission on Racially Motivated
          Violence and to examine the prevalence of violence
          against members of minority groups.

          June 21. The U.S. Senate Committee on the Judiciary
          holds hearings to consider proposed legislation to re-
          quire the U.S. Justice Department to collect and publish
          statistics on hate crimes.
              Tom Trimble and Lloyd Griffen, two gay men, are
          gruesomely murdered in a Dallas, Texas, park by
          Richard Lee Bednarski.

1989   January 17. Patrick Purdy enters an elementary school yard in Stockton, California, and fires 105 rounds from an AK-47, killing three Cambodian girls, Ram Chun, Sokhim An, and Oeun Lim; a Cambodian boy, Rathanan Or; and a Vietnamese girl, Thuy Tran. The gunman also wounds 30 others, including the teacher. He then kills himself. The 24-year-old had an obsessive hatred of Cambodians, Indians, Pakistanis, and especially Vietnamese.

July 29. Two brothers in Raleigh, North Carolina, beat to death Ming Hai "Jim" Loo, a 24-year-old Chinese American. Witnesses told police that the men thought Loo was Vietnamese and that their brother served in the U.S. military in Vietnam and never returned.

August 23. A white gang armed with baseball bats and guns attack four black youths on a street in Bensonhurst, a neighborhood in Brooklyn, New York. Yusuf Hawkins is beaten and shot to death in the attack. Seven perpetrators are arrested.

1990   January 21. James Zappalorti, a gay Vietnam war veteran, is brutally murdered in Staten Island, New York, by two teenagers.

March 15. Henry Lau, a 31-year-old Chinese immigrant, is fatally stabbed on a New York City subway train. Prior to the stabbing, the assailant called Lau an "eggroll."

April 23. President George Bush signs into law the Hate Crime Statistics Act, which requires the FBI to compile annual statistics on hate crimes throughout the United States.

August 9. Two skinheads shouting "white power" murder Hung Truong, a 15-year-old Vietnamese youth in Houston.

1991   March 3. Rodney King, an African American motorist, is beaten by four white Los Angeles police officers after a routine traffic stop. The incident is captured on videotape by a bystander and gains national media attention.

1991   August 19. Following a traffic accident that killed Gavin
cont.   Cato, a 7-year-old African American, black youths mur-
        der Yankel Rosenbaum, a visiting Australian Jewish
        scholar. During three days of rioting in the Crown
        Heights section of Brooklyn, crowds roam the streets
        yelling, "Get the Jews."

1992   April 29. A jury in suburban Simi Valley, California ac-
        quits four white Los Angeles police officers on all but
        one charge stemming from the beating of black motorist
        Rodney King in March 1991.

        April 30–May 3 Following the controversial jury verdict,
        the south central section of Los Angeles is engulfed in
        widespread burning, looting, and violence. Fifty-eight
        people are killed in the rioting and damage estimates
        range as high as $1 billion. According to Yumi Park, for-
        mer director of the Korean American Grocers Associa-
        tion, 800 Korean-owned establishments were damaged.
        Tensions between African Americans and Korean Amer-
        icans had risen following the November 15, 1991 trial of
        Soon Ja Du, a Korean grocer who had shot to death a 15-
        year-old black girl, Latasha Harlins. Even though the
        grocer was convicted of manslaughter, the judge had re-
        fused to send her to prison.

        May 11. The U.S. House of Representatives Committee
        on the Judiciary holds hearings on crimes motivated by
        prejudice against the racial, ethnic, religious, or sexual
        orientation of the victim.

        June 22. In the case of *R. A. V. v. City of St. Paul,* the U.S.
        Supreme Court strikes down a hate crime ordinance in
        St. Paul, Minnesota.

        July 29. The U.S. House of Representatives Committee
        on the Judiciary holds hearings on the use of penalty en-
        hancement for hate crimes and also examines the impli-
        cations of the June 22 U.S. Supreme Court decision.

        August 5. The U.S. Senate Committee on the Judiciary re-
        views implementation of the Hate Crime Statistics Act of
        1990 by the FBI, state crime reporting agencies, and local

law enforcement agencies under the direction of the U.S. Department of Justice.

August 18. Luyen Phan Nguyen, a 19-year-old premed student at the University of Miami, is beaten to death by five men in Coral Springs, Florida, who made disparaging remarks about his Vietnamese ancestry.

October 27. Seaman Allen Schindler, serving on a U.S. Navy ship, is brutally murdered by a shipmate outside a military base in Japan. The assailant had recently learned of Schindler's homosexuality.

1993   January. The Federal Bureau of Investigation releases its first official report containing nationwide hate crime statistics for 1991.
      The National Asian Pacific American Legal Consortium issues its first *Audit of Violence Against Asian Pacific Americans.*

June 11. The U.S. Supreme Court unanimously upholds Wisconsin's penalty enhancement hate crimes statute in the case *Wisconsin v. Mitchell.*

November 16. The U.S. House of Representatives Committee on the Judiciary discusses proposed legislation that would make crimes of violence motivated by gender actionable under civil rights and hate crime laws.

December 7. Colin Ferguson, a black Jamaican immigrant, murders Mi Kyung Kim, James Gorycki, Dennis McCarthy, Marita Theresa Magtoto, Amy Federici, and Richard Nettleton on the Long Island Railroad. He had previously written notes expressing hatred of Asians and whites.

1994   March 1. Rashid Baz, a Lebanese immigrant, shoots at a van carrying 15 Hasidic Jewish students over the Brooklyn Bridge. One student, Aaron Halberstam, is killed; another, Nachum Sasonkin, is severely injured. The murderer once vowed to "kill all Jews."

September 1. A mosque in Yuba City, California, is gutted in a suspected anti-Muslim arson case.

1994   September 13. The Violent Crime Control and Law En-
cont.   forcement Act directs the United States Sentencing Com-
        mission to devise sentencing guidelines to incorporate a
        federal sentence enhancement for hate crimes.

        The Violence Against Women Act (Title IV of the Vio-
        lent Crime Control Act) provides civil rights remedies for
        gender-motivated violence, explicitly stating that all
        "persons within the United States shall have the right to
        be free from crimes of violence motivated by gender."

1995   December 7. Michael Jones and Jackie Burden, two
        African Americans, are murdered in a random shooting
        by soldiers from Fort Bragg, North Carolina, affiliated
        with white supremacist groups.

        December 8. Roland Smith, who had previously picketed
        a Jewish-owned store in Harlem, enters the store and
        shoots four people and then douses the premises with
        lighter fluid. The ensuing blaze kills seven people: Gar-
        nette Ramautar, Mayra Rentas, Cynthia Martinez, An-
        gelina Marrero, Luz Ramos, Kareem Brunner, and Olga
        Garcia. The gunman-arsonist also died.

1996   January 29. Thien Minh Ly, a 24-year-old Vietnamese
        American, is kicked, stomped, and stabbed more than a
        dozen times on a tennis court in Tustin, California, in a
        racially motivated attack by white skinheads.

        June 25. The U.S. House of Representatives Committee
        on National Security holds hearings on the participation
        of current or former U.S. military personnel in antigov-
        ernment or racist hate groups.

        June 27. The U.S. Senate Committee on the Judiciary
        holds hearings on the rash of arsons directed against
        black churches and other acts of violence against houses
        of worship.

1997   February 23. Ali Abu Kamal, a 69-year-old Palestinian
        teacher who arrived in the U.S. in December 1996, opens
        fire on the 86th floor observation deck of the Empire
        State Building in New York City, killing a Danish tourist
        and wounding six others before taking his own life. In a

pouch around Abu Kamal's neck, police found a letter stating his intention: to kill as many "Zionists" as possible in their "den" in New York City.

November 18. Oumar Dia, an immigrant from Mauritania, is murdered at a Denver, Colorado, bus stop by Nathan Thill, a skinhead, who later said he hated blacks. (Dia, a black African, had fled his native country because he was persecuted by Arabs.) Jeannie Vanvelkinburgh, a white woman who came to his aid, was also shot and became paralyzed from the waist down.

1998   February 23. Members of the New Order, a neo-Nazi group, are arrested in their homes in southern Illinois, where police found guns, pipe bombs, and hand grenades. The FBI said the suspects were plotting to bomb the Southern Poverty Law Center in Montgomery, Alabama, and the Simon Wiesenthal Center, the New York headquarters of the Anti-Defamation League. Authorities learned of the plot when the suspects attempted to recruit a man who then became a federal informant.

Also on February 23, in the largest hate crime judgment in Illinois history, a jury awards $6 million to the family of Ricardo Arroyo of Waukegan, Illinois, who died from injuries inflicted by another motorist. After their cars collided, Arroyo was kicked in the stomach three times and the assailant shouted, "Mexicans, go back to Mexico!"

March 13. Brian Wilmes falls into a coma after being beaten outside of a San Francisco, California, gay bar by an attacker who uttered antihomosexual slurs. In November 1998, a municipal court judge ruled that the alleged assailant, Edgard Mora, must stand trial for murder with a hate crime enhancement.

April 5. Five white men in Orange County, California, are beaten by five Iranian males attending an Iranian New Year's party. They jumped behind the victims—whose names were not released by police—yelling, "What are you white guys doing here?" A witness captures the attack on videotape, including a perpetrator with steel-toed boots kicking a victim.

1998
cont.

April 14. In Biddeford, Maine, Anthony Cabana is sent to jail for threatening to "snap" a woman's neck. He is reportedly the first person ever charged in Maine with a gender-based hate crime.

April 27. Steven Goedersis, a gay man, is brutally beaten to death in Fort Lauderdale, Florida. His teenage murderers are being prosecuted under the Florida hate crime statute.

May 9. In Rutherfordton, North Carolina, two men with Ku Klux Klan ties attack Isaiah Edgerton, his wife, and 2-year-old daughter in their house. The men, both in their twenties, are charged with a hate crime. Police suspect that the local chapter of the American Knights of the KKK ordered the shooting.

May 20. A cross is burned in front of a Jewish family's home in Huntington Beach, California. It is the second anti-Jewish crime committed against the family; in an earlier incident, someone stamped a swastika on their front lawn.

June 7. James Byrd Jr., a 49-year-old black man, is chained to a pickup truck in Jasper, Texas, and dragged along an asphalt road for almost two miles. His head, neck, and right arm are found on the road. His attackers, who claimed membership in the white supremacist group Aryan Nation, reportedly said to Byrd, "We're starting the *Turner Diaries* early." This book, widely disseminated among white racists and neo-Nazis, advocates the murder of African Americans and Jews. President Bill Clinton issues a statement condemning the grisly murder. On February 23, 1999, a jury of eleven whites and one black convicts John William King, one of the perpetrators, of murder. He is sentenced to death by lethal injection.

September 20. In the South Ozone Park neighborhood of Queens, New York, Rishi Maharaj, the 21-year-old son of Trinidadan immigrants of Indian decent, is beaten by three young men who utter anti-Indian slurs. He suffers severe head trauma, facial fractures, and other injuries. The Queens district attorney condemns the incident as an unprovoked hate crime and charges the assailants with attempted murder.

October 6. Matthew Shepard, a gay college student in Laramie, Wyoming, is tied to a fence and savagely beaten with a gun by two men he met in a bar. Left for dead, he is found by a passerby 18 hours later. He remains in a coma for several days and dies October 12. His funeral is protested by the Reverend Fred Phelps and his followers from Topeka, Kansas, who carry signs saying "God hates fags" and "Fags deserve to die."

October 12–15. President Clinton condemns the murder of Matthew Shepard; the U.S. House of Representatives passes a resolution condemning the murder as a hate crime.

December 19. Vandals shatter windows at two synagogues and disfigure a lighted menorah in Sharon, Massachusetts, during the seventh day of Hanukkah. Local police call the incidents hate crimes.

1999   January 21. Miami University of Ohio police arrest two black students after finding their fingerprints on antiblack racist flyers that were posted on October 30, 1998 at the university's Center for Black Culture and Learning. The leaflets sparked two days of campus demonstrations from students protesting racist attitudes at the university. According to the January 8, 1999, issue of the *Chronicle of Higher Education*, students on at least five other campuses fabricated hate crimes in the previous 18 months.

February 19. Billy Jack Gaither, a gay man in Sylacauga, Alabama, is bludgeoned to death with an axe and his body burned on a pyre of tires. Steven Mullins and Charles Butler Jr. are arrested after claiming to have plotted Gaither's murder because he "made a pass" at them.

Biographical Sketches 3

Much of the available information on hate crimes and hate groups comes from the research and publications of human rights activists, college professors, journalists, and authors. Because their work often involves exposing the activities of violent individuals and groups, some human rights activists prefer to remain out of the public eye. Their wishes have been respected, and they have not been included in this chapter. Following are brief biographies of some notable experts on hate crimes.

Chip Berlet (1949–)

A senior analyst at Political Research Associates, Chip Berlet has written widely during the past 25 years about extreme right-wing groups, theocratic fundamentalism, and American right-wing populism. In 1985, he cofounded the Public Eye BBS, the first computer bulletin board system designed to challenge the information circulated by the KKK and the neo-Nazis.

Berlet has written op-ed pieces for many publications, including the *New York Times, Boston Globe,* and *Tikkun* magazine. He is the editor of the anthology *Eye's Right: Challenging the Right-Wing Backlash* (Boston:

South End Press, 1995). He has appeared on ABC's *Nightline*, the NBC *Today Show*, and *CBS This Morning* and has spoken at academic conferences, including the American Sociological Association. A longtime critic of the extremist ideologue Lyndon LaRouche, Berlet has been sued twice by the LaRouche movement for his characterization of them as a conspiracist neo-Nazi movement engaged in illegal fundraising activities. LaRouche's organization lost both cases.

In the late 1970s and early 1980s, Berlet helped expose a white racist and anti-Semitic coalition trying to organize farm groups. During that time, he and his wife lived in the Chicago neighborhood of Marquette Park; they organized community groups to fight racist hate crimes, including the firebombing of black homes, in the area.

Following the 1995 bombing of the federal building in Oklahoma City, Berlet was retained by CNN as an expert commentator and was also interviewed by other national media outlets. In 1996, he received an award from the Arkansas-based Gustavus Myers Center for the Study of Human Rights in North America.

Kathleen M. Blee (1953–)

A sociology and women's studies professor at the University of Pittsburgh, Kathleen Blee has written widely on the sociology of racism and gender. Her book *Women of the Klan: Racism and Gender in the 1920s* (Berkeley: University of California Press, 1991) won an award from the Gustavus Myers Center for the Study of Human Rights in North America. The work discusses the little-known fact that women in the 1920s constituted almost half of the Klan membership in some states and, even more surprisingly, that these women were simultaneously involved in such progressive movements as women's suffrage.

Currently, Blee is the director of the Women's Studies Program at the University of Pittsburgh. Prior to this position, she taught at the University of Kentucky and did extensive research on poverty in eastern Kentucky. She is currently working on a book on women in organized hate movements.

Floyd Cochran (1956–)

Born in rural Cortland, New York, Floyd Cochran came from a troubled background—a common upbringing of many individuals later involved in racist hate movements. His mother was jailed for armed robbery and his father physically abused him. He was later placed in a foster home.

Early on, Cochran developed an interest in Nazism and Adolph Hitler. After high school, he became a member of the Ku Klux Klan. He married and soon divorced after having two sons.

In 1990, he moved to the Pacific Northwest and became active in the Aryan Nation, the largest U.S. neo-Nazi group, with headquarters in northern Idaho. He soon became a major spokesman for the group, recruiting skinheads and other disaffected individuals.

"In six months," he once boasted, "I went from milking cows in upstate New York to being in *Newsweek*. There are very few racists who could smile and make hatred sound as palatable as I could."

At a 1992 youth festival, however, he was shocked when he heard someone talking about killing disabled people. His son, then four years old, was born with a cleft palate. He soon left the movement and eventually met with two individuals who had formerly been his most bitter adversaries: Lenny Zeskind and Loretta Ross, a Jewish man and an African American woman who work with the Center for Democratic Renewal.

After several meetings with Zeskind and Ross, Cochran eventually renounced his racist and anti-Semitic views. He soon emerged as a leading national speaker warning against the dangers of racist hate movements. Currently, he tours the country speaking at civic groups and on radio and television. He recounts his odyssey with these groups, especially aiming his message at susceptible young people. Cochran recalls indoctrinating one youth who was later convicted of firebombing the Tacoma, Washington, office of the NAACP.

Although his life has been repeatedly threatened by his former comrades, Cochran has given more than 100 public talks during the past few years. He often ends his speeches with a heartfelt sentiment: "If my racism harmed you in any way, directly or indirectly, I am sorry."

Rabbi Abraham Cooper (1950–)

The associate dean of the Simon Wiesenthal Center in Los Angeles, Rabbi Cooper came to California with Rabbi Marvin Hier to help establish the institution in 1977. A graduate of Yeshiva University, he has been a long-time activist for human and Jewish rights throughout the world. His extensive involvement in the Soviet Jewry movement included visiting refuseniks in the 1970s, helping to open the Jewish Cultural Center in Moscow in the 1980s, and lecturing at the Soviet Academy of Sciences and the Sakharov Foundation in the 1990s.

Since the early 1980s, Rabbi Cooper has administered the Wiesenthal Center's international agenda on worldwide anti-Semitism, Nazi war criminals, violent extremist groups, and hate on the Internet. In July 1992, he helped coordinate an international conference on anti-Semitism cosponsored by the United Nations Educational, Scientific, and Cultural Organization (UNESCO) and the Simon Wiesenthal Center. He later testified before the United Nations, which established the Wiesenthal Center as a non-governmental organization (NGO) at the world body. In 1997, Cooper coordinated the Simon Wiesenthal Center's international conference entitled *Property and Restitution—The Moral Debt to History*, which was held in Geneva, Switzerland.

Cooper regularly travels to Asia to counter the proliferation of anti-Semitic stereotypes, including lecturing in Japan, South Korea, and the People's Republic of China. He arranged national broadcasts of the Wiesenthal Center's documentary *Genocide* on Chinese and Russian television. Later, he arranged for a special Japanese language exhibit on Anne Frank and the Holocaust.

As the associate dean of the center, Cooper supervised the research and production of the Interactive Learning Center on the Holocaust and World War II for the Beit Hashoah Museum of Tolerance. This unique learning center has compiled more than 12,000 separate entries by historians and scholars, 50,000 photographs culled from archives in a dozen countries, and rare historical film footage. The rabbi has helped administer the Wiesenthal Center web site and made special presentations about the extremist use of the Internet before the United Nations Commission on Human Rights and the Pentagon, among other institutions.

Cooper is the editor-in-chief of *Response,* the center's quarterly publication, and is contributing editor of PAGE ONE, its weekly on-line magazine.

Morris Dees (1936–)

The son of an Alabama farmer, Morris Dees gave up a successful career running a mail order and book publishing business to pursue his commitment to civil rights. A graduate of the University of Alabama Law School, he filed suit in 1967 to stop construction of a white university in an Alabama city that had a predominantly black state college. A year later, he brought a lawsuit to integrate the all-white Montgomery YMCA.

In 1971, Dees and his law partner, Joseph I. Levin Jr., along with Julian Bond founded the Southern Poverty Law Center. Currently, he is chief trial counsel and chair of the Executive Committee of the Southern Poverty Law Center. He has received several awards for his work, including the Martin Luther King Jr. Memorial Award from the National Education Association and the Roger Baldwin Award from the American Civil Liberties Union.

In addition to his work against hate groups, Dees has been active with the Democratic Party. In 1972, he was the finance director of Senator George McGovern's presidential campaign and also performed similar duties for Governor Jimmy Carter in 1976 and Senator Edward Kennedy in 1980.

In 1991, Dees published his autobiography, *A Season for Justice*. His second book, *Hate on Trial: The Case Against America's Most Dangerous Neo-Nazi* (New York: Villard Books, 1993), chronicles the trial and $12.5 million judgment against white supremacist Tom Metzger and his White Aryan Resistance group for their responsibility in the brutal beating and death of an Ethiopian student in Portland, Oregon. His latest work, *Gathering Storm: America's Militia Threat* (New York: HarperCollins, 1996), exposes contemporary domestic terrorist organizations.

Steven Emerson (1954–)

A former senior editor of *U.S. News and World Report* and staff member of the U.S. Senate Foreign Relations Committee, Emerson is one of the leading national authorities on terrorist movements, intelligence issues, and the Middle East. He has written *The American House of Saud* (New York: Franklin Watts, 1985) and coauthored *Fall of Pan Am 103: Inside the Lockerbie Investigation* (New York: Putnam, 1990) and *Terrorist: The Inside Story of the Highest Ranking Iraqi Ever to Defect to the West* (New York: Villard Books, 1991).

His highly praised PBS documentary, "Jihad in America," which won the George Polk Award for best documentary, aired in November 1994. This show exposed the growth of Islamic terrorist organizations in the United States. Although Emerson has persistently made a clear distinction between Islamic radicals and the vast majority of nonviolent Muslims, some critics have charged him with causing "anti-Muslim hate crimes." However, his documentary interviews Muslims also worried about radical Islamic groups, and the show states that these terrorist groups do not represent the precepts of Islam.

In late 1995, federal law enforcement officials notified Emerson that a terrorist squad had entered the United States and was planning to assassinate him, yet Emerson has not been deterred in his work by the threats of terrorist groups. He has worked at CNN and is currently affiliated with an investigative group uncovering international and domestic links to world-wide terrorism.

Gail Gans

Gail Gans is director of the Anti-Defamation League of B'nai B'rith's Fact Finding Department and was formerly associate director of the Research and Evaluation Department. She began her career with the ADL reading and evaluating right-wing extremist hate literature in the Research Department. She was assistant to the Fact Finding Director for four years before rejoining the Research Department. Gans has been working with the ADL for 20 years.

A graduate of the University of Illinois, she has previously held newspaper and publishing jobs in both Illinois and New York City. Gans has done research and written extensively on hate groups such as the Ku Klux Klan, neo-Nazis, and other extremist organizations.

David Goldman (1963–)

The developer of HateWatch, Goldman founded this major web-based organization that monitors the increasing activity of hate groups on the Internet. Started in 1996, HateWatch provides an important on-line resource for concerned individuals, academics, activists, and the media.

Goldman produces a weekly Internet radio show entitled "The State of Hate" and has organized electronic listservs for individuals wanting to discuss on-line hate movements. He has written articles on the dissemination of hate literature on the Internet and spoke at the B'nai B'rith International Symposium on Hate Groups on the Internet in Toronto, Canada, in 1997. He has attended several conferences on the topic and was a guest lecturer at Wayne State University, speaking on "Hate Groups on the Internet: Confrontation and Containment."

Gregory Herek

Gregory Herek is a research psychologist at the University of California at Davis and has written widely on prejudice against lesbians and gay men and antigay violence. In 1992, he coedited *Hate Crimes: Confronting Violence Against Lesbians and Gay Men* with Kevin Berrill (Newbury Park, Calif.: Sage Publications). In 1986 he testified on the topic of antigay violence on behalf of the American Psychological Association at a hearing of the U.S. House of Representatives Criminal Justice Subcommittee. Herek was also a participant at the White House Conference on Hate Crime in November 1997. He has served as a consultant and expert witness for many legal cases involving the civil rights of lesbians and gay men, including recent cases challenging U.S. military personnel policy.

James B. Jacobs (1947–)

The director of the Center for Research in Crime and Justice at New York University Law School, Jacobs is a leading critic of hate crimes legislation. He has written widely on the topic in many law and academic journals, including *The Journal of Criminal Law & Criminology, Annual Survey of American Law, Criminal Justice Ethics,* and *Public Interest.*

His first book, *Statesville: The Penitentiary in Mass Society* (Chicago: University of Chicago Press, 1977), is still used in university classrooms throughout the country. Jacobs is the coauthor with Kimberly Potter of *Hate Crimes: Criminal Law and Identity Politics* (New York: Oxford University Press, 1998).

Mark Potok (1955–)

As director of publications and information for the Southern Poverty Law Center's Klanwatch Project, Potok is frequently interviewed in the national media about extreme right-wing violence and hate movements. Before joining Klanwatch, Potok was the southwest correspondent for *USA Today,* covering the siege in Waco, Texas; the Oklahoma City bombing; and the trial of Timothy McVeigh. Potok has also worked at the *Dallas Times Herald* and the *Miami Herald*. Currently, he coordinates media relations for Klanwatch and edits their newsletter, *Intelligence Report.*

Kenneth Stern (1953–)

An attorney for the American Jewish Committee since 1989, Stern has written about hate on talk radio, bigotry on campuses, and Holocaust denial. His report, *Militias: A Growing Danger,* was issued two weeks before the Oklahoma City bombing. Stern is also the author of *Liberators: A Background Report* (New York: American Jewish Committee, 1993), an investigative study of a PBS documentary about U.S. Army soldiers who liberated Nazi concentration camps. His report questioned the accuracy of the film; PBS later withdrew this documentary from distribution. He also wrote *Holocaust Denial,* an early work on the dissemination of lies spread by anti-Semitic propagandists on the Nazi Holocaust. His books include *Loud Hawk* (Norman: University of Oklahoma Press, 1994), which surveys prejudice against Native Americans, and *A Force Upon the Plain: The American Militia Movement and the Politics of Hate* (New York: Simon and Schuster, 1996).

In his capacity as an attorney for the American Jewish Committee, Stern has written legal briefs, including an appeal of the Leonard Jeffries case, and served as counsel on the committee brief in the landmark U.S. Supreme Court case *Wisconsin v. Mitchell*. (See Chapter 4 for information on this case.)

In 1997, Stern served as a presenter at the White House Conference on Hate Crimes. He has also served as director of the National Organization Against Terrorism, a project working to support American victims of international terrorism.

Lu-In Wang

Professor Wang is the author of the preeminent legal text on hate crime, *Hate Crimes Law* (Deerfield, Ill.: Clark Boardman Callaghan, 1994, updated annually). This work is consulted by attorneys, legal scholars, and researchers needing to find authoritative information on the topic. Her approach is interdisciplinary, treating legal, sociological, and psychological aspects of the subject. In addition, she has written on violence and the law.

Wang is an assistant professor of law at the University of Pittsburgh School of Law and a member of the Illinois and Michigan bar.

Statistics and Documents

Statistics

Hate Crime Statistics Act of 1990

After debating the issue of hate crimes for some time, Congress passed the Hate Crime Statistics Act and President George Bush signed it into law on April 23, 1990. This legislation requires the Justice Department to collect data on crimes that "manifest prejudice based on race, religion, sexual orientation, or ethnicity." Since the FBI started issuing these annual reports in 1993, the number of law enforcement agencies collecting and analyzing data on hate crimes has grown substantially. Although some Congressional critics believed that the gathering of these statistics might unduly magnify the issue, several human rights groups believe the FBI has underreported bigoted crimes directed at various minority groups. Nevertheless, the FBI annual report has proved to be an important governmental mechanism for monitoring and publicizing hate crimes.

§ 534. Acquisition, preservation, and exchange of identification records and information; appointment of officials

(a) The Attorney General shall—

(1) acquire, collect, classify, and preserve identification, criminal identification, crime, and other records;

(2) acquire, collect, classify, and preserve any information which would assist in the identification of any deceased individual who has not been identified after the discovery of such deceased individual;

(3) acquire, collect, classify, and preserve any information which would assist in the location of any missing person (including an unemancipated person as defined by the laws of the place of residence of such person) and provide confirmation as to any entry for such a person to the parent, legal guardian, or next of kin of that person (and the Attorney General may acquire, collect, classify, and preserve such information from such parent, guardian, or next of kin);

(4) exchange such records and information with, and for the official use of, authorized officials of the Federal Government, the States, cities, and penal and other institutions.

(b) The exchange of records and information authorized by subsection (a)(4) of this section is subject to cancellation if dissemination is made outside the receiving departments or related agencies.

(c) The Attorney General may appoint officials to perform the functions authorized by this section.

(d) For purposes of this section, the term "other institutions" includes—

(1) railroad police departments which perform the administration of criminal justice and have arrest powers pursuant to a State statute, which allocate a substantial part of their annual budget to the administration of criminal justice, and which meet training requirements established by law or ordinance for law enforcement officers; and

(2) police departments of private colleges or universities which perform the administration of criminal justice and have arrest powers pursuant to a State statute, which allocate a substantial part of their annual budget to the administration of criminal justice, and which meet training requirements established by law or ordinance for law enforcement officers.

(e)(1) Information from national crime information databases consisting of identification records, criminal history records, protection orders, and wanted person records may be disseminated to civil or criminal courts for use in domestic violence or stalking cases. Nothing in this subsection shall be construed to permit access to such records for any other purpose.

(2) Federal and State criminal justice agencies authorized to

enter information into criminal information databases may include—

(A) arrests, convictions, and arrest warrants for stalking or domestic violence or for violations of protection orders for the protection of parties from stalking or domestic violence; and

(B) protection orders for the protection of persons from stalking or domestic violence, provided such orders are subject to periodic verification.

(3) As used in this subsection—

(A) the term "national crime information databases" means the National Crime Information Center and its incorporated criminal history databases, including the Interstate Identification Index; and

(B) the term "protection order" includes an injunction or any other order issued for the purpose of preventing violent or threatening acts or harassment against, or contact or communication with or physical proximity to, another person, including temporary and final orders issued by civil or criminal courts (other than support or child custody orders) whether obtained by filing an independent action or as a *pendente lite* order in another proceeding so long as any civil order was issued in response to a complaint, petition, or motion filed by or on behalf of a person seeking protection.

FBI Hate Crime Report, 1996

Section I

Hate Crime Statistics, 1996

During 1996, 8,759 bias-motivated criminal incidents were reported to the FBI by 11,354 law enforcement agencies in 49 states and the District of Columbia. Of the 8,759 incidents, 5,396 were motivated by racial bias; 1,401 by religious bias; 1,016 by sexual-orientation bias; 940 by ethnicity/ national origin bias; and 6 by multiple biases. The 8,759 incidents involved 10,706 separate offenses, 11,039 victims, and 8,935 known offenders. (See Table 1.) Sixty-nine percent of the incidents involved only one per-individual (person) victim, while 94 percent involved a single offense type.

Offenses

Crimes against persons composed 69 percent of the 10,706 offenses reported. Intimidation was the single most frequently reported hate crime among all offenses measured, accounting for 39 percent of the total. Following were destruction/ damage/ vandalism of property, 27 percent; simple assault, 16 percent; and aggravated assault, 13 percent. (See Table 3.)

Twelve persons were murdered in 1996 in incidents motivated by hate. Racial bias motivated the highest number of these murders, 8. Bias against Hispanics served as the motivation for 2 of the 12 homicides, while sexual-orientation bias motivated the remaining 2. (See Table 4.) When examining incidents of racial bias, 2,647 of the 4,469 antiblack offenses involved white offenders, while 818 of the 1,384 antiwhite offenses involved black offenders. (See Table 5.)

Victims

Eight of every 10 of the 11,039 reported hate crime victims were individuals (people), while the remaining were businesses, religious organizations, or various other targets. In 1996, 67 percent of the 11,039 victims were targets of crimes against persons. (See Table 3.) Six of every 10 victims were attacked because of their race, with bias against blacks accounting for 42 percent of the total. (See Table 1.) Of the total number of victims of religious bias crimes, 66 percent of victims were targets of crimes against property. (See Table 9.) Hate crimes committed because of religious bias are more likely to be against property rather than against persons.

Offenders

Law enforcement agencies reported 8,935 known offenders to be associated with the 8,759 incidents recorded in 1996. Of the known offenders, 66 percent were white and 20 percent were black. (See Table 11.) Unlike victims and/or witnesses of crimes against property, those who witness or are victimized by crimes against persons are frequently able to assist with identifying the offenders. Thirty-eight percent of the known offenders were reported in connection with the offense of intimidation. (See Table 3, footnote 1.) Offenders were unknown for 3,490 or 40 percent of the incidents. Offenders of religious bias crimes are difficult to identify because most of the crimes they commit are against property. Clearance rates are historically low for these types of crimes. Law enforcement identified only 523 offenders in connection with 1,401 religious bias incidents in 1996. (See Table 1.)

Locations

In 1996, the majority of hate crime incidents, 31 percent, occurred in/on residential properties. Following closely were incidents perpetrated on highways/roads/ alleys/streets, accounting for 21 percent, while 9 percent occurred at schools/colleges. The remaining incidents were widely distributed among various locations. (See Table 2.)

TABLE 1
Number of Incidents, Offenses, Victims, and Offenders by Bias Motivation, 1996

	Number of Incidents	Offenses	Victims	Known Offenders
Total	8,759	10,706	11,039	8,935
Single Bias Incidents				
Race:	5,396	6,767	6,994	6,122
Anti-White	1,106	1,384	1,445	1,783
Anti-Black	3,674	4,469	4,600	3,701
Anti-American Indian/Alaskan Native	51	69	71	56
Anti-Asian/Pacific Islander	355	527	544	374
Anti-Multi-Racial Group	210	318	334	208
Ethnicity/National Origin:	940	1,163	1,207	1,095
Anti-Hispanic	564	710	728	734
Anti-Other Ethnicity/National Origin	376	453	479	361
Religion:	1,401	1,500	1,535	523
Anti-Jewish	1,109	1,182	1,209	371
Anti-Catholic	35	37	38	17
Anti-Protestant	75	80	81	44
Anti-Islamic	27	33	33	16
Anti-Other Religious Group	129	139	145	64
Anti-Multi-Religious Group	24	27	27	11
Anti-Atheism/Agnosticism/etc.	2	2	2	0
Sexual Orientation:	1,016	1,256	1,281	1,180
Anti-Male Homosexual	757	927	940	925
Anti-Female Homosexual	150	185	192	150
Anti-Homosexual	84	94	99	93
Anti-Heterosexual	15	38	38	4
Anti-Bisexual	10	12	12	8
Multiple-Bias Incidents	6	20	22	15[1]

[1]There were six multiple-bias incidents. Within these incidents there were 20 offenses, 22 victims, and 15 known offenders.

TABLE 2
Location of Incidents by Bias Motivation, 1996

	Total Incidents	Race[1]	Ethnicity/ National Origin	Religion	Sexual Orientation
Total	8,759	5,402	940	1,401	1,016
Air/bus/train terminal	83	61	7	4	11
Bank/savings and loan	15	12	1	1	1
Bar/night club	141	79	11	3	48
Church/synagogue/temple	321	56	4	255	6
Commercial office building	232	152	15	37	28
Construction site	27	22	2	3	0
Convenience store	85	51	20	8	6
Department/discount store	39	28	7	0	4
Drugstore/Dr.'s office/hospital	37	19	7	10	1
Field/woods	101	66	11	11	13
Government/public building	90	55	7	17	11
Grocery/supermarket	54	35	10	2	7
Highway/road/alley/street	1,832	1,305	192	73	262
Hotel/motel/etc.	44	22	11	4	7
Jail/prison	36	26	5	1	4
Lake/waterway	12	6	3	0	3
Liquor store	10	9	0	0	1
Parking lot/garage	445	307	53	26	59
Rental storage facility	1	1	0	0	0
Residence/home	2,734	1,692	309	415	318
Restaurant	190	110	39	13	28
School/college	799	543	60	118	78
Service/gas station	61	39	11	3	8
Specialty store (TV, fur, etc.)	164	91	13	51	9
Other/unknown	1,191	604	140	346	101
Multiple locations	15	11	2	0	2

[1]Includes six multiple-bias incidents listed in Table 1. All these incidents involved racial bias as a part of multiple-hate motivation.

TABLE 3

Number of Offenses, Victims, and Offenders by Offense, 1996

	Number of Offenses	Victims	Known Offenders
Total	10,706	11,039	10,021[1]
Crimes against Persons:	7,359	7,359	8,132
Murder	12	12	21
Forcible Rape	10	10	20
Aggravated Assault	1,444	1,444	2,150
Simple Assault	1,762	1,762	2,566
Intimidation	4,130	4,130	3,374
Other[2]	1	1	1
Crimes against Property:	3,330	3,663	1,868
Robbery	155	205	355
Burglary	140	161	84
Larceny-theft	75	77	49
Motor Vehicle Theft	7	9	1
Arson	75	87	56
Destruction/Damage/Vandalism	2,874	3,120	1,312
Other[2]	4	4	11
Crimes against Society:[2]	17	17	21

[1]The actual number of known offenders is 8,935. (See Table 1.) Some offenders, however, committed more than one offense per incident and are, therefore, counted more than once in this table.

[2]Includes offenses other than those listed that are collected in NIBRS.

TABLE 4
Number of Offenses by Bias Motivation and Offense Type, 1996

Crimes Against Persons	Total Offenses	Murder	Forcible Rape	Aggravated Assault	Simple Assault	Intimidation	Other[1]
Total	10,706	12	10	1,444	1,762	4,130	1
Single Bias Incidents							
Race:	6,767	8	9	1,004	1,219	2,712	1
Anti-White	1,384	1	5	281	430	399	0
Anti-Black	4,469	5	4	599	676	1,880	1
Anti-American Indian/ Alaskan Native	69	0	0	17	14	30	0
Anti-Asian/Pacific Islander	527	1	0	60	64	273	0
Anti-Multi-Racial Group	318	1	0	47	35	130	0
Ethnicity/National Origin:	1,163	2	1	182	211	494	0
Anti-Hispanic	710	2	1	123	147	290	0
Anti-Other Ethnicity/ National Origin	453	0	0	59	64	204	0
Religion:	1,500	0	0	34	39	442	0
Anti-Jewish	1,182	0	0	18	26	363	0
Anti-Catholic	37	0	0	0	1	9	0
Anti-Protestant	80	0	0	2	1	9	0
Anti-Islamic	33	0	0	1	0	25	0
Anti-Other Religious Group	139	0	0	10	10	28	0
Anti-Multi-Religious Group	27	0	0	3	1	8	0
Anti-Atheism/Agnosticism/etc.	2	0	0	0	0	0	0
Sexual Orientation:	1,256	2	0	222	287	472	0
Anti-Male Homosexual	927	2	0	188	225	334	0
Anti-Female Homosexual	185	0	0	21	45	70	0
Anti-Homosexual	94	0	0	11	12	35	0
Anti-Heterosexual	38	0	0	1	1	29	0
Anti-Bisexual	12	0	0	1	4	4	0
Multiple Bias Incidents[2]	20	0	0	2	6	10	0

Crimes Against Property	Robbery	Burglary	Larceny-theft	Motor Vehicle Theft	Arson	Destruction/ Damage/ Vandalism	Other[1]	Crimes Against Society[1]
Total	15	140	75	7	75	2,874	4	17
Single Bias Incidents								
Race:	93	74	44	3	38	1,549	2	11
Anti-White	60	13	15	1	2	174	1	2
Anti-Black	26	48	21	1	33	1,169	0	6
Anti-American Indian/ Alaskan Native	1	0	0	0	0	7	0	0
Anti-Asian/Pacific Islander	5	6	5	1	1	111	0	0
Anti-Multi-Racial Group	1	7	3	0	2	88	1	3
Ethnicity/National Origin:	28	17	5	1	7	209	2	4
Anti-Hispanic	17	9	5	0	3	112	0	1

[1]Includes offenses other than those listed that are collected in NIBRS.
[2]There were six multiple-bias incidents. Within these incidents there were 20 offenses.

TABLE 4 *continued*

	Robbery	Burglary	Larceny-theft	Motor Vehicle Theft	Arson	Destruction/ Damage/ Vandalism	Other[1]	Crimes Against Society[1]
Anti-Other Ethnicity/ National Origin	11	8	0	1	4	97	2	3
Religion:	3	42	14	2	22	901	0	1
Anti-Jewish	2	19	7	0	10	737	0	0
Anti-Catholic	1	3	2	0	1	20	0	0
Anti-Protestant	0	8	1	0	6	53	0	0
Anti-Islamic	0	1	0	0	0	6	0	0
Anti-Other Religious Group	0	8	4	2	5	71	0	1
Anti-Multi-Religious Group	0	1	0	0	0	14	0	0
Anti-Atheism/Agnosticism/etc.	0	2	0	0	0	0	0	0
Sexual Orientation:	31	6	12	0	8	215	0	1
Anti-Male Homosexual	27	3	5	0	6	136	0	1
Anti-Female Homosexual	2	1	5	0	1	40	0	0
Anti-Homosexual	2	2	0	0	1	31	0	0
Anti-Heterosexual	0	0	1	0	0	6	0	0
Anti-Bisexual	0	0	1	0	0	2	0	0
Multiple Bias Incidents	0	1	0	1	0	0	0	0

[1]Includes offenses other than those listed that are collected in NIBRS.

TABLE 5
Number of Offenses by Bias Motivation and Suspected Offender's Race, 1996

	Total Offenses	White	Black	American Indian/ Alaskan Native	Asian/ Pacific Islander	Multi-Racial Group	Unknown
Single Bias Incidents							
Race:	6,767	3,334	995	40	71	116	2,211
Anti-White	1,384	219	818	21	25	42	259
Anti-Black	4,469	2,647	103	13	32	42	1,632
Anti-American Indian /Alaskan Native	69	46	8	1	1	0	13
Anti-Asian/Pacific Islander	527	291	44	5	13	9	165
Anti-Multi-Racial Group	318	131	22	0	0	23	142
Ethnicity/National Origin:	1,163	625	100	7	17	14	400
Anti-Hispanic	710	425	71	5	12	5	192
Anti-Other Ethnicity/ National Origin	453	200	29	2	5	9	208
Religion:	1,500	260	24	1	9	4	1,202
Anti-Jewish	1,182	189	15	1	5	2	970
Anti-Catholic	37	11	1	0	1	0	24
Anti-Protestant	80	18	0	0	0	0	62
Anti-Islamic	33	6	1	0	0	0	26
Anti-Other Religious Group	139	32	4	0	2	2	99
Anti-Multi-Religious Group	27	4	3	0	1	0	19
Anti-Atheism/Agnosticism/etc.	2	0	0	0	0	0	2
Sexual Orientation:	1,256	659	139	2	9	39	408
Anti-Male Homosexual	927	532	108	2	9	34	242
Anti-Female Homosexual	185	73	27	0	0	4	81
Anti-Homosexual	94	44	4	0	0	0	46
Anti-Heterosexual	38	6	0	0	0	0	32
Anti-Bisexual	12	4	0	0	0	1	7
Multiple Bias Incidents[1]	20	14	0	0	0	4	2

[1]There were six multiple-bias incidents. Within these incidents there were 20 offenses.

TABLE 6
Number of Offenses by Suspected Offender's Race, 1996

			SUSPECTED OFFENDER'S RACE				
	Total Offenses	White	Black	American Indian/ Alaskan Native	Asian/ Pacific Islander	Multi- Racial Group	Unknown
Total	10,706	4,892	1,258	50	106	177	4,223
Crimes against Persons:	7,359	4,221	1,078	42	91	157	1,770
Murder	12	8	4	0	0	0	0
Forcible Rape	10	6	4	0	0	0	0
Aggravated Assault	1,444	907	304	8	32	51	142
Simple Assault	1,762	1,127	425	20	28	59	103
Intimidation	4,130	2,173	341	14	31	47	1,524
Other[1]	1	0	0	0	0	0	1
Crimes against Property:	3,330	665	177	8	14	16	2,450
Robbery	155	67	61	1	4	2	20
Burglary	140	24	8	0	0	0	108
Larceny-theft	75	24	4	2	1	1	43
Motor Vehicle Theft	7	0	1	0	0	0	6
Arson	75	29	7	0	0	0	39
Destruction/Damage/Vandalism	2,874	519	96	5	9	12	2,233
Other[1]	4	2	0	0	0	1	1
Crimes against Society:[1]	17	6	3	0	1	4	3

[1]Includes offenses other than those listed that are collected in NIBRS.

TABLE 7
Percent Distribution of Offenses by Victim Type, 1996

			VICTIM TYPE			
	Total[1]	Individual	Business/ Financial Institution	Government	Religious Organization	Society/ Public	Other/ Unknown/ Multiple
Total	100	84	3	1	2	3	6
Crimes against Persons:	100	100	NA	NA	NA	NA	NA
Crimes against Property:	100	50	9	3	8	10	20
Robbery	100	99	1	0	0	0	0
Burglary	100	52	10	1	14	6	17
Larceny-theft	100	77	10	0	6	2	6
Motor Vehicle Theft	100	100	0	0	0	0	0
Arson	100	46	5	1	25	5	17
Destruction/Damage/Vandalism	100	46	10	4	7	12	22
Other[2]	100	50	25	25	0	0	0
Crimes against Society:[2]	100	NA	NA	NA	NA	100	NA

[1]Because of rounding, the percentages may not add to total.
[2]Includes offenses other than those listed that are collected in NIBRS.

TABLE 8
Number of Offenses by State, 1996

	Total Offenses	Murder	Forcible Rape	Aggravated Assault	Simple Assault	Intimidation	Other[1]
CRIMES AGAINST PERSONS							
Total	10,706	12	10	1,444	1,762	4,130	1
Alabama	0	0	0	0	0	0	0
Alaska	13	0	0	1	1	8	0
Arizona	294	0	3	41	57	112	0
Arkansas	1	1	0	0	0	0	0
California	2,723	4	2	476	472	1,117	0
Colorado	168	0	0	16	27	87	0
Connecticut	161	0	0	22	22	60	0
Delaware	80	0	0	9	5	20	0
District of Columbia	16	0	0	7	4	2	0
Florida	215	0	1	64	44	37	0
Georgia	32	0	0	8	10	3	0
Idaho	91	0	0	21	28	13	0
Illinois	450	0	0	69	125	147	0
Indiana	48	0	0	4	8	28	0
Iowa	54	0	0	11	8	18	0
Kansas	38	0	0	5	7	22	0
Kentucky	139	1	0	23	21	49	0
Louisiana	25	0	0	1	3	20	0
Maine	78	0	0	1	12	48	0
Maryland	431	0	0	60	67	68	0
Massachusetts	523	1	0	53	40	232	0
Michigan	565	0	1	73	140	171	1
Minnesota	320	0	1	35	63	142	0
Mississippi	3	0	0	1	0	1	0
Missouri	229	1	0	58	46	92	0
Montana	16	0	0	3	7	2	0
Nebraska	3	0	0	2	1	0	0
Nevada	45	0	0	7	11	14	0
New Hampshire	1	0	0	0	1	0	0
New Jersey	947	1	0	30	84	414	0
New Mexico	54	0	0	10	21	8	0
New York	920	1	0	82	15	420	0
North Carolina	40	0	0	4	2	13	0
North Dakota	2	0	0	0	1	0	0
Ohio	282	0	0	11	63	132	0
Oklahoma	100	1	0	20	14	36	0
Oregon	194	0	0	27	30	93	0
Pennsylvania	250	0	1	16	28	122	0
Rhode Island	51	0	0	4	5	25	0
South Carolina	69	0	0	30	10	15	0
South Dakota	3	0	0	0	2	0	0
Tennessee	42	0	0	2	8	15	0

TABLE 8 *continued*

CRIMES AGAINST PERSONS

	Total Offenses	Murder	Forcible Rape	Aggravated Assault	Simple Assault	Intimidation	Other[1]
Texas	439	0	1	74	132	129	0
Utah	73	0	0	9	23	10	0
Vermont	5	0	0	0	3	1	0
Virginia	107	0	0	6	11	23	0
Washington	280	1	0	41	49	130	0
West Virginia	4	0	0	0	0	1	0
Wisconsin	78	0	0	6	31	29	0
Wyoming	4	0	0	1	0	1	0

CRIMES AGAINST PROPERTY

	Robbery	Burglary	Larceny-theft	Motor Vehicle Theft	Arson	Destruction/ Damage/ Vandalism	Other[1]	Crimes Against Society[1]
Total	155	140	75	7	75	2,874	4	17
Alabama	0	0	0	0	0	0	0	0
Alaska	0	0	0	0	0	3	0	0
Arizona	2	6	0	1	2	70	0	0
Arkansas	0	0	0	0	0	0	0	0
California	60	44	15	3	18	512	0	0
Colorado	3	1	1	0	1	32	0	0
Connecticut	1	2	0	0	1	53	0	0
Delaware	1	4	1	0	3	37	0	0
District of Columbia	0	0	0	0	0	3	0	0
Florida	5	6	0	0	5	53	0	0
Georgia	1	0	0	0	0	10	0	0
Idaho	1	1	1	0	1	25	0	0
Illinois	5	2	0	0	4	98	0	0
Indiana	0	0	0	0	1	7	0	0
Iowa	1	0	1	0	1	14	0	0
Kansas	1	0	0	0	0	3	0	0
Kentucky	3	3	0	0	3	36	0	0
Louisiana	0	1	0	0	0	0	0	0
Maine	1	1	1	0	0	14	0	0
Maryland	5	3	2	0	2	224	0	0
Massachusetts	4	1	3	0	0	188	0	1
Michigan	12	13	21	3	4	113	2	11
Minnesota	2	3	3	0	4	67	0	0
Mississippi	0	0	0	0	0	1	0	0
Missouri	0	1	1	0	0	30	0	0
Montana	0	0	0	0	0	4	0	0
Nebraska	0	0	0	0	0	0	0	0
Nevada	1	2	0	0	0	10	0	0
New Hampshire	0	0	0	0	0	0	0	0
New Jersey	5	6	4	0	6	397	0	0

TABLE 8 *continued*

CRIMES AGAINST PROPERTY

	Robbery	Burglary	Larceny-theft	Motor Vehicle Theft	Arson	Destruction/ Damage/ Vandalism	Other[1]	Crimes Against Society[1]
New Mexico	0	2	0	0	0	13	0	0
New York	20	15	5	0	6	356	0	0
North Carolina	1	0	0	0	2	18	0	0
North Dakota	0	0	0	0	0	0	1	0
Ohio	2	0	0	0	0	74	0	0
Oklahoma	0	1	1	0	2	25	0	0
Oregon	0	4	1	0	1	38	0	0
Pennsylvania	1	2	1	0	1	78	0	0
Rhode Island	1	0	0	0	0	16	0	0
South Carolina	1	1	2	0	1	9	0	0
South Dakota	0	0	0	0	0	1	0	0
Tennessee	0	1	0	0	0	16	0	0
Texas	8	6	2	0	4	83	0	0
Utah	0	0	5	0	0	20	1	5
Vermont	0	0	0	0	0	1	0	0
Virginia	1	2	2	0	1	61	0	0
Washington	5	6	2	0	1	45	0	0
West Virginia	0	0	0	0	0	3	0	0
Wisconsin	1	0	0	0	0	11	0	0
Wyoming	0	0	0	0	0	2	0	0

[1]Includes offenses other than those listed that are collected in NIBRS.

TABLE 9
Number of Victims by Bias Motivation and Offense Type, 1996

CRIMES AGAINST PERSONS

	Total Victims	Murder	Forcible Rape	Aggravated Assault	Simple Assault	Intimidation	Other[1]
Total	11,039	12	10	1,444	1,762	4,130	1
Single Bias Incidents							
Race:	6,994	8	9	1,004	1,219	2,712	1
Anti-White	1,445	1	5	281	430	399	0
Anti-Black	4,600	5	4	599	676	1,880	1
Anti-American Indian/ Alaskan Native	71	0	0	17	14	30	0
Anti-Asian/Pacific Islander	544	1	0	60	64	273	0
Anti-Multi-Racial Group	334	1	0	47	35	130	0
Ethnicity/National Origin:	1,207	2	1	182	211	494	0
Anti-Hispanic	728	2	1	123	147	290	0
Anti-Other Ethnicity/ National Origin	479	0	0	59	64	204	0
Religion:	1,535	0	0	34	39	442	0
Anti-Jewish	1,209	0	0	18	26	363	0
Anti-Catholic	38	0	0	0	1	9	0
Anti-Protestant	81	0	0	2	1	9	0
Anti-Islamic	33	0	0	1	0	25	0
Anti-Other Religious Group	145	0	0	10	10	28	0
Anti-Multi-Religious Group	27	0	0	3	1	8	0
Anti-Atheism/Agnosticism/etc.	2	0	0	0	0	0	0
Sexual Orientation:	1,281	2	0	222	287	472	0
Anti-Male Homosexual	940	2	0	188	225	334	0
Anti-Female Homosexual	192	0	0	21	45	70	0
Anti-Homosexual	99	0	0	11	12	35	0
Anti-Heterosexual	38	0	0	1	1	29	0
Anti-Bisexual	12	0	0	1	4	4	0
Multiple Bias Incidents[2]	22	0	0	2	6	10	0

CRIMES AGAINST PROPERTY

	Robbery	Burglary	Larceny-theft	Motor Vehicle Theft	Arson	Destruction/ Damage/ Vandalism	Other[1]	Crimes Against Society[1]
Total	205	161	77	9	87	3,120	4	17
Single Bias Incidents								
Race:	131	89	46	4	46	1,712	2	11
Anti-White	90	18	15	1	2	200	1	2
Anti-Black	32	52	22	1	41	1,281	0	6
Anti-American Indian/ Alaskan Native	2	0	0	0	0	8	0	0
Anti-Asian/Pacific Islander	6	11	6	2	1	120	0	0
Anti-Multi-Racial Group	1	8	3	0	2	103	1	3

TABLE 9 *continued*

CRIMES AGAINST PROPERTY

	Robbery	Burglary	Larceny-theft	Motor Vehicle Theft	Arson	Destruction/ Damage/ Vandalism	Other[1]	Crimes Against Society[1]
Ethnicity/National Origin:	37	19	5	1	8	241	2	4
Anti-Hispanic	24	11	5	0	3	121	0	1
Anti-Other Ethnicity/ National Origin	13	8	0	1	5	120	2	3
Religion:	3	44	14	2	24	932	0	1
Anti-Jewish	2	21	7	0	12	760	0	0
Anti-Catholic	1	3	2	0	1	21	0	0
Anti-Protestant	0	8	1	0	6	54	0	0
Anti-Islamic	0	1	0	0	0	6	0	0
Anti-Other Religious Group	0	8	4	2	5	77	0	1
Anti-Multi-Religious Group	0	1	0	0	0	14	0	0
Anti-Atheism/Agnosticism/etc.	0	2	0	0	0	0	0	0
Sexual Orientation:	34	7	12	0	9	235	0	1
Anti-Male Homosexual	27	4	5	0	6	148	0	1
Anti-Female Homosexual	2	1	5	0	2	46	0	0
Anti-Homosexual	5	2	0	0	1	33	0	0
Anti-Heterosexual	0	0	1	0	0	6	0	0
Anti-Bisexual	0	0	1	0	0	2	0	0
Multiple Bias Incidents[2]	0	2	0	2	0	0	0	0

[1]Includes offenses other than those listed that are collected in NIBRS.
[2]There were six multiple-bias incidents. Within these incidents there were 22 victims.

TABLE 10
Percent Distribution of Bias Motivation by Victim Type, 1996

			VICTIM TYPE			
	Total[1]	Individual	Business/ Financial Institution	Government	Religious Organization	Society/ Public	Other/ Unknown/ Multiple[1]
Racial	100	87	3	1	1	3	5
Ethnicity/National Origin	100	90	3	0	0	3	4
Religion	100	50	8	1	15	8	18
Sexual Orientation	100	92	1	1	0	2	5
Multiple Bias	100	100	0	0	0	0	0

[1]Because of rounding, the percentages may not add to total.

TABLE 11
Number of Known Offenders by Race, 1996

NUMBER OF KNOWN OFFENDERS	
Total	8,935
Suspected Offender's Race:	
White	5,891
Black	1,826
American Indian/Alaskan Native	48
Asian/Pacific Islander	157
Multi-Racial Group	339
Unknown Race	674

TABLE 12
Agency Hate Crime Reporting by State, 1996[1]

Participating States	Number of Participating Agencies	Agencies Population Covered	Total Number Submitting Incident Reports	Number of Incidents Reported
Total	11,354	223,346,702	1,834	8,759
Alabama	289	4,167,898	0	0
Alaska	1	254,774	1	9
Arizona	81	4,253,428	19	250
Arkansas	191	2,510,000	1	1
California	718	31,502,681	256	2,052
Colorado	230	3,820,118	27	133
Connecticut	98	2,772,165	44	114
Delaware	50	724,747	9	67
District of Columbia	1	543,000	1	16
Florida	394	14,658,195	51	187
Georgia	2	413,123	2	28
Idaho	112	1,202,496	32	72
Illinois	113	5,412,562	113	348
Indiana	179	3,634,883	12	36
Iowa	231	2,841,077	25	43
Kansas	1	312,706	1	28
Kentucky	527	3,848,633	49	109
Louisiana	140	2,697,770	5	6
Maine	131	1,235,309	10	58
Maryland	148	5,071,690	37	387
Massachusetts	405	6,091,117	102	454
Michigan	485	7,958,039	159	486
Minnesota	307	4,648,824	58	268
Mississippi	129	1,716,566	3	3
Missouri	230	4,270,323	25	150
Montana	95	858,174	4	10
Nebraska	10	207,564	2	3
Nevada	4	1,169,351	3	44
New Hampshire	2	81,381	1	1
New Jersey	568	7,995,838	273	839
New Mexico	70	1,298,291	8	44
New York	499	17,645,588	40	903
North Carolina	83	2,888,221	19	34
North Dakota	101	640,486	2	2
Ohio	405	8,873,634	55	234
Oklahoma	293	3,294,345	27	83
Oregon	174	3,155,762	27	172
Pennsylvania	1,137	11,833,651	43	205
Rhode Island	46	990,000	11	40
South Carolina	340	3,677,033	24	42
South Dakota	32	255,844	2	3
Tennessee	191	2,904,931	13	33
Texas	915	19,026,891	88	350
Utah	124	1,988,036	25	59
Vermont	3	35,462	3	4
Virginia	409	6,678,025	32	100
Washington	230	5,466,381	62	198
West Virginia	22	179,467	3	4
Wisconsin	338	5,160,000	21	43
Wyoming	70	480,222	4	4

[1]Due to the updating of Hate Crime submissions, data in this table may differ from those published in the 1996 edition of *Crime in the United States*.

Section II

Nearly 11,400 law enforcement agencies provided 1 to 12 months of hate crime reports during 1996 to the FBI's UCR Program. The number of reporting agencies by state, along with the corresponding population coverage, is shown in Table 12. Also indicated is the number of agencies recording hate crimes during 1996, as well as the number of incidents reported by those jurisdictions.

The individual jurisdictional figures are presented in six tables delineating city, rural county, suburban county, universities and colleges, state law enforcement agencies, and other agencies. The tables give the number of reported crimes motivated by bias against race, ethnicity, religion, and sexual orientation. Of the agencies that participated in the hate crime program, 16 percent reported that at least one hate crime occurred in their jurisdiction, while the other 84 percent reported that none occurred.

Due to the many factors affecting the nature and volume of crime, care must be exercised in making any comparisons among agencies, even where agencies reported for similar timeframes. All factors must be considered before valid comparisons can be achieved.

Hate Crime in California, 1996

Issued by the Office of the Attorney General in California, this report covers the period January 1–December 31, 1996. It is the third report submitted to the California State Legislature regarding crimes motivated by the victim's race, ethnicity, religion, sexual orientation, or physical or mental disability. Since California is the largest state in the country comprising a multiethnic and culturally diverse population, excerpts from this report are included as a model for disseminating statistical and other information on hate crimes.

I. Message from the Attorney General

1996 was the second full year California has collected statewide data to document the number of crimes committed each year motivated by the victims' race, ethnicity, religion, sexual orientation or physical or mental disability. We commonly refer to these acts as "hate crimes" and with good reason. They are crimes which are committed with the particularly ugly notion in mind: that the victim is less of a human being than the perpetrator, that by virtue of mere individual differences the victim is not entitled to the protection of the rights enshrined in our Constitution for all men and women.

Those who are victimized by hate crimes suffer enormous pain. The damage extends, however, to our whole society as well. This is especially true for California, our nation's most diverse state.

Local law enforcement agencies are responding to this problem through increased community interaction and community-oriented policing strategies. In August 1995, I established the Anti–Hate Violence Project, which allows local agencies which may lack sufficient evidence to bring criminal charges against a person for an alleged hate crime, to bring a civil lawsuit through the Attorney General's Civil Rights Enforcement Unit. Combined with the state's tough sentencing enhancements for those convicted of hate-motivated felonies and the "Three Strikes and You're Out" law, we have every reason to hope that California will continue to be a place where respect for all people is the societal norm.

California's modern heritage is one in which diversity is respected, not scorned. As long as hate crimes continue to counter that heritage, the men and women of law enforcement are pledged to intercede on behalf of all Californians.

Daniel E. Lungren, Attorney General

II. Overview

The Attorney General's Hate Crime Reporting Program was implemented in 1994. In 1995, the first publication, *Hate Crime in California, July through December 1994,* was issued. The second yearly publication, *Hate Crime in California, 1995,* and this publication, *Hate Crime in California, 1996,* include data for January through December.

As defined in California Penal Code section 13023, a hate crime is any criminal act or attempted criminal act motivated by hatred based on race, religion, ethnicity, sexual orientation or disability. These crimes must be reported to the Department of Justice (DOJ) by law enforcement agencies. Information about bias-motivation, type of crime, location of crime, number of victims, and number of known suspects is included in each crime report.

All law enforcement agencies in California participate in this program. These agencies recognize that quality information is central to developing effective measures to deal with hate crime. In cooperation with the DOJ, agencies in California have initiated local data collection programs which include quality control measures. The results of these data collection efforts are presented in this publication.

Data Comparison—A Cautionary Note

Data resulting from new reporting programs should be collected for several years in order that statistical data can be properly analyzed. Because of this, the DOJ does not recommend comparing these 1996 data with previously published data. In addition, the DOJ believes that data reported for 1995 and 1996 may be underreported. Future reporting will improve as law enforcement personnel are trained to identify, investigate, and report hate crimes.

A number of additional factors can influence the volume of hate crime reported to the DOJ. These are:

• Efforts of community groups and law enforcement hate crime networks to identify and report hate crime to appropriate authorities

• Cultural practices and likeliness of reporting hate crime

• Strength and investigative emphasis of law enforcement agencies

• Policies of law enforcement and prosecutorial agencies

• Community policing policies

III. Introduction

California Penal Code Section 13023 requires the Attorney General to submit an annual report to the Legislature regarding crimes motivated by the victim's race, ethnicity, religion, sexual orientation or physical or mental disability as reported by law enforcement agencies. Data collection began in the fall of 1994 after an orientation and training period. Agencies were requested to identify and submit all reports of bias-motivated crime occurring on or after July 1, 1994, to the Department of Justice. In 1995, the Department of Justice published its first report covering data reported for July through December 1994. This is the third report and covers the period January 1 through December 31, 1996.

Since this is a relatively new program and long-term comparative information is not available, caution is advised in interpreting the data. As program participants gain experience in identifying, documenting, interpreting, aggregating and displaying the information, statistical data will become available that will provide a basis for annual trend analysis and policy development.

IV. Background

In January 1986, the California Department of Justice (DOJ) submitted a report to the Legislature in response to Senate Bill 2080 (Watson). This report, entitled *Racial, Ethnic, and Religious Crime Project, Preliminary Steps to Establish Statewide Collection of Data*, recommended:

• The Department of Justice be designated as the appropriate state agency to implement and coordinate statewide bias-motivated crime data collection.

• Law enforcement agencies submit existing crime reports identified as bias-motivated to the DOJ.

• Uniform definitions and guidelines be established to ensure reliable and consistent identification of bias-motivated crimes.

• Adequate funding be provided for data collection and local law enforcement agency training.

Senate Bill 202 (Watson) was chaptered in 1989. The bill added Section 13023 to the Penal Code requiring the Attorney General, subject to the availability of funding, to begin collecting and reporting bias-motivated crime information.

The federal "Hate Crime Statistics Act," Public Law 101–275 which became law on April 23, 1990, required the United States Attorney General to collect bias-motivated crime information. The FBI began collecting the data from volunteer agencies in 1991. The first report was published in 1992.

After funding for the California program was obtained, agencies were notified by Information Bulletin 94–25-OMET issued September 30, 1994, to begin reporting bias-motivated crimes to the DOJ.

Information Bulletin 95–09-BCIA, issued March 24, 1995, requested California district attorneys to report information on complaints filed and convictions for bias-motivated crimes on a standard form.

V. Methodology

Following the recommendations in the 1986 report, the DOJ requires each law enforcement agency in the state to submit copies of bias-motivated crime reports on a monthly basis. To ensure relevancy to the subject matter, the DOJ requests that each agency establish a two-tier review process of possible bias-motivated incidents before reports are forwarded.

Reports received by the DOJ are reviewed by at least two members of the bias-motivated crime unit before the data are included in the aggregate reports. All crime reports that meet the bias-motivated criteria are coded in a standard format by the DOJ staff. If the report is not complete or if it appears that the incident is not bias-motivated, the agency is notified.

VI. Policing Agency Data

A. Definitions

Bias—A preformed negative opinion or attitude toward a group of persons based on their race, religion, ethnicity/national origin, sexual orientation and/or physical/mental disability.

Racial bias—A preformed negative opinion or attitude toward a group of persons, such as Asian, blacks, or whites, based on common physical characteristics.

Ethnic bias—A preformed negative opinion or attitude toward a group of persons of the same race or national origin that share common or similar traits such as languages, customs, and traditions, for example Arabs or Hispanics.

Religious Bias—A preformed negative opinion or attitude toward a group of persons that share the same religious beliefs regarding the origin and purpose of the universe and the existence or nonexistence of a supreme being, such as Catholics, Jews, Protestants or Atheists.

Sexual orientation bias—A preformed negative opinion or attitude toward a group of persons based on sexual preferences and/or attractions toward and responsiveness to members of their own or opposite sexes.

Physical/mental disability bias—A preformed negative opinion or attitude toward a group of persons based on physical or mental impediments/challenges, whether such disabilities are congenital or acquired by heredity, accident, injury, advanced age, or illness.

Event—An event is an occurrence where a hate crime is involved. In this report the information about the event is a crime report or source document that meets the criteria for a hate crime. There may be one or more suspects involved, one or more victims targeted, and one or more offenses involved for each event.

Offenses—Offenses that are recorded are: murder, forcible rape, robbery, aggravated assault, burglary, larceny-theft, motor vehicle theft, arson, simple assault, intimidation, and destruction/damage/vandalism as defined in the national Uniform Crime Report (UCR) and the national Hate Crimes Statistics Report.

Violent crimes—Murder, forcible rape, robbery, aggravated assault, simple assault and intimidation are considered violent crimes in this report. (Robbery is included in crimes against property in the FBI Hate Crimes Statistics Report.)

Property crimes—Burglary, larceny-theft, motor vehicle theft, arson, and destruction/vandalism are reported as property crimes.

Victim—A victim may be an individual, a business or financial institution, an organization or the society/public in general. For example, if a church or synagogue is vandalized and/or desecrated, the victim would be a religious organization.

Known suspect(s)—A suspect can be any person alleged to have committed a criminal act(s) or attempted a criminal act(s) to cause physical injury, emotional suffering, or property damage. The known suspect category contains the number of suspects that have been identified and/or alleged to have committed hate crimes as stated in the crime report. For example, witnesses observe three suspects fleeing the scene of a crime. The word "known" does not necessarily refer to specific identities.

Location—The place where the hate crime event occurred. The location categories follow UCR location specifications. Examples are residence, hotel, bar, church, etc.

B. Highlights

• For 1996, the Department of Justice received reports detailing 2,054 hate crime events. Included in these events were 2,321 offenses, 2,529 victims, and 2,441 known suspects.

• 71.2 percent of the events occurred because of the race/ethnicity of the victim.

• Violent crimes accounted for 74.5 percent of known offenses.

• 35.9 percent of the hate crimes occurred at a residence or the home of the victim.

VII. Prosecution Data

A. Definitions

Relationship between "complaints filed" and "convictions"—The annual survey questionnaire used to collect these data reports the total number of hate crime cases filed and the total number of hate crime convictions. There is no direct relationship since a case may be filed in one period and the trial outcome may occur in another.

Case—A case is a set of facts about a crime that is referred to a district attorney for filing with a court. The case may charge one or more persons with the commission of one or more offenses. For this report, the case must contain some element of bias.

Complaints filed—Any verified written accusation, filed by a district attorney with a criminal court, that charges one or more persons with the commission of one or more offenses. For this report, the case must contain some element of bias.

Conviction—A conviction is a judgment based either on the verdict of a jury or a judicial officer or on a guilty plea of the defendant.

Guilty plea—A guilty plea or answer by a person accused of a crime which indicates that he or she is guilty of the crime with which he or she is charged.

Nolo contendere—A plea or answer in a criminal action in which the accused does not admit guilt but agrees to be subject to the same punishment as if he or she were guilty.

Trial verdict—The finding or answer of a jury or judge concerning a matter submitted to them for their judgment.

VIII. Data Information and Limitations

A. Law Enforcement

Local law enforcement agencies are required to submit monthly copies of hate crime reports to the Department of Justice (DOJ) in compliance with Section 13023 of the Penal Code which states ". . . any criminal acts or attempted criminal acts to cause physical injury, emotional suffering, or property damage where there is a reasonable cause to believe that the crime was motivated, in whole or in part, by the victim's race, ethnicity, religion, sexual orientation, or physical or mental disability . . ." shall be reported to DOJ.

In 1995, the Bias-Motivated Crime File contained a total of 2,054 events defined as bias-motivated crimes received from reporting California law enforcement agencies.

The following information and limitations should be considered when using the bias-motivated crime data:

1. The hate crime reporting system was implemented by DOJ in September 1994. Law enforcement agencies were requested to submit copies of initial crime reports beginning with July 1994. Crime reports that were submitted as bias-motivated but later determined to be unfounded were not included.

2. Initial crime reports were selected as the reporting document to provide maximum information for coding and to minimize the workload impact on local law enforcement agencies.

3. The aggregated data are designed to identify the motivation of the perpetrator of the crime. Due to the subjectivity that may be involved in identifying motivation, caution is advised in interpreting the data.

4. The data differ somewhat from that collected by the FBI for the National Program (Public Law 101–275-April 23, 1990). Physical or mental disability has not been part of the FBI definition of a bias-motivated crime but is included in the definition in California legislation (P.C. 13023) and has now been added to the FBI reporting program (effective January 1, 1997).

5. The Department of Justice requested that each law enforcement agency establish procedures incorporating a two-tier review (decision-making) process. The first level is done by the initial officer who responds to the suspected hate crime incident. At the second level, each report is reviewed by at least one other officer to confirm that the incident was, in fact, a bias-motivated crime.

6. Caution should be used when making jurisdictional comparisons. Factors to be considered are: cultural diversity and population density, effective strength of law enforcement agencies, and training in identification of hate crimes by law enforcement.

7. The Department of Justice shall submit to the Legislature the results of the information obtained from law enforcement agencies.

8. All requests or questions regarding these data should be submitted to the Criminal Justice Statistics Center, P.O. Box

903427, Sacramento, California 94203–4270. The E-mail address is cjsc@hdcdojnet.state.ca.us.

B. District Attorneys

The 1996 District Attorney's Report File of Hate Crime Cases contains a total of 149 complaints filed and 122 convictions. Thirty-two district attorneys had no hate crime cases filed by their offices during the period.

The following information and limitations should be considered when interpreting the bias-motivated cases:

1. In order to show the criminal justice system's response to bias-motivated crimes, in March of 1995, the Attorney General requested all district attorneys to submit summary data of complaints filed and convictions.

2. The 1995 District Attorney's Report File of Bias-Motivated Cases contains summary data based on cases referred to each district attorney, filings and convictions which occurred between January 1, 1996 through December 31, 1996.

3. All requests or questions regarding these data should be submitted to the Criminal Justice Statistics Center, P.O. Box 903427, Sacramento, California 94203–4270. The E-mail address is cjsc@hdcdojnet.state.ca.us.

C. City Attorneys

There are nine elected city attorneys in California. Eight out of the nine prosecute misdemeanor bias-motivated cases.

The following information and limitations should be considered when interpreting and using the city attorney's summary report of bias-motivated cases:

1. In order to show the criminal justice system's response to bias-motivated crimes, in March of 1995, the Hate Crime Unit at the DOJ requested all elected city attorneys to submit summary data of bias-motivated crime complaints filed and convictions.

2. The 1996 City Attorney's Report File of Bias-Motivated Cases contains summary data based on cases referred to each city attorney, filings and convictions which occurred between January 1, 1996 through December 31, 1996.

3. All requests or questions regarding these data should be submitted to the Criminal Justice Statistics Center, P.O. Box 903427, Sacramento, California 94203–4270. The E-mail address is dlesac@ns.net.

IX. Guidelines for the Identification of Hate Crimes

A reportable hate crime is any criminal act or attempted criminal act to cause physical injury, emotional suffering, or property damage which is or appears to be motivated, all or in part, by the victim's race, ethnicity, religion, sexual orientation, physical or mental disability.

Initial review of a suspected hate crime should consider the following factors:

• Is the motivation of the offender known?

• Are the victim and the offender from different racial, religious, ethnic, sexual orientation, or is the victim targeted because of his or her physical or mental disability?

• Were any racial, religious, ethnic, sexual orientation, physical or mental disability bias remarks made by the offender?

• Were there any offensive symbols, words or acts that are known to represent a hate group or other evidence of bias against the victim's group?

• Does the victim perceive the action of the offender to have been motivated by bias?

• Did the incident occur on a holiday or other day of significance to the victim's group or the offender's group?

• What do the demographics of the area tell you about the incident—was the victim in an area where the predominant population is dissimilar to the victim's group?

• Is there no clear other motivation for the incident?

Second level of review before making the final determination of whether an incident was motivated by bias:

• Is the victim a member of a targeted racial, religious, ethnic, sexual orientation, physical or mental disability group?

• Has the victim or victim's group been subjected to repeat attacks of a similar nature?

• Does a substantial portion of the community where the crime occurred perceive that the incident was motivated by bias?

• Would the incident have taken place if the victim and offender were the same race, religion, ethnic group, sexual orientation, physical or mental disability?

X. Laws and Reporting Information

Laws and regulations governing the reporting of hate crimes in California are as follows:

California Penal Code Section 13023. Senate Bill No. 2080,

Chapter 1482 (Sept. 25, 1984). Public Law 101–275 (April 23, 1990). Department of Justice Information Bulletin #94–25 (Sept. 30, 1994). Department of Justice Information Bulletin #95–09 (March 24, 1995).

Government Documents

Issued by the Clinton Administration, these press statements provide information on the U.S. government's active program to combat hate-motivated violence.

President Clinton: Getting Tough on Hate Crime

President Announces Significant New Law Enforcement and Prevention Initiatives

> Hate crimes . . . leave deep scars not only on the victims, but on our larger community. They weaken the sense that we are one people with common values and a common future. They tear us apart when we should be moving closer together. They are acts of violence against America itself.
> . . . As part of our preparation for the new century, it is time for us to mount an all-out assault on hate crimes, to punish them swiftly and severely, and to do more to prevent them from happening in the first place. We must begin with a deeper understanding of the problem itself.

The White House Conference on Hate Crimes

On November 10, 1997, the President convened the first-ever White House Conference on Hate Crimes, a day-long event held at The George Washington University. At the Conference, the President announced significant law enforcement and prevention initiatives to get tough on hate crimes. The Conference examined the positive actions that communities are taking and outlined the steps we all can take to prevent hate crimes.

A hate crime is the embodiment of intolerance—an act of violence against a person or property based on the victim's race, color, gender, national origin, religion, sexual orientation or disability. Every year, thousands of Americans are victims of hate crimes—and it is suspected that many more go unreported.

Teenagers and young adults account for a significant proportion of the country's hate crimes—both as perpetrators and victims. Every time one of these crimes is committed it creates tension and fear, and tears at the fabric of community life.

The Conference is an important element of the President's Initiative on Race and of his vision for One America. Members of the President's Advisory Board on Race participated in the Conference at satellite locations.

President Clinton: Getting Tough on Hate Crimes

The President, Vice President, Attorney General and Secretary of Education were joined by other members of the Cabinet, Members of Congress, selected state and local officials, and approximately 350 leaders from the law enforcement, civil rights, anti-violence, youth, education, and religious communities.

Hate crimes survivors attended. Participants included representatives from all 50 states. Thousands more participated at over 50 satellite-linked events across the country.

Conference Schedule and Location

The President hosted a breakfast for Conference participants at the White House and made an opening address at the Conference. After his remarks, the President chaired a panel discussion in which the Attorney General, the Secretary of Education, and several other distinguished Americans joined.

In the afternoon, members of the Cabinet and other senior Administration officials chaired a number of concurrent working sessions to examine various aspects of the hate crimes issue. Afterward, the Attorney General chaired a closing panel to discuss ideas and themes from the working sessions. Participants attended a closing reception at the United States Holocaust Museum.

The Clinton Administraton: Drawing a Line Against Hate Crimes

The Clinton Administration: Fighting Hate in Our Communities

• In Richland, Mississippi, four members of a neo-Nazi skinhead organization pled guilty to conspiracy and interfering with the housing rights of an interracial couple by throwing a molotov cocktail at their trailer home.

• Three defendants, one of whom is a racist skinhead and a member of the white supremacist group South Bay Nazi Youth, were convicted of a civil rights conspiracy after they drove through the streets of Lubbock, Texas, hunting African-American men, luring them to the conspirators' car, and shooting the men at close range with a short-barreled shotgun. One victim died, one was seriously wounded in the face, and another had a finger blown off.

• In Livingston, Texas, six defendants pled guilty to civil rights charges for beating randomly selected African-American men with a rifle and a rodeo belt buckle, and punching them repeatedly as they tried to escape. The defendants had been angered at seeing other black men in the presence of white women.

• In Livermore Falls, Maine, two defendants pled guilty to civil rights charges after firing shots at the Latino victims' fleeing car, wounding one victim in the arm. [Source: Department of Justice, Civil Rights Division, October 1997]

Fighting Hate Crimes Through Tough Law Enforcement

Vigorously Prosecuting Hate Crimes Under the Civil Rights Statutes. Several federal statutes provide jurisdiction to prosecute hate crimes—crimes where the perpetrator selects his victim on the basis of certain characteristics such as race, color, religion, and national origin. Since 1989, over 500 defendants in more than half of the 50 states have been convicted on federal criminal civil rights charges for interfering with various federally protected rights of minority victims. Virtually all defendants charged in these cases have been convicted. President Clinton's Justice Department has vigorously prosecuted hate crime incidents, including where the defendants were members of organized hate groups, such as the Ku Klux Klan and various skinhead gangs.

Enhanced Penalties For Hate Crimes. As part of the historic 1994 Crime Act, the President signed the Hate Crimes Sentencing Enhancement Act which provides for longer sentences where the offense is determined to be a hate crime. In 1996 alone, 27 cases received enhanced sentences.

The Bureau of Alcohol, Tobacco and Firearms (ATF) Provides Expertise in Arson and Explosives Investigations to Help Fight Hate Crimes Throughout America. While enforcing explosives and arson laws over which it has jurisdiction, ATF has participated in the investigations of bombing and arson incidents triggered by animus against characteristics such as race and sexual orientation. The ATF, for example, has investigated the bombing of predominantly gay bars and nightclubs.

Sensible Gun Regulation Helps Stem the Flow Of Firearms that Can Fuel Hate Group Activity. Many organized hate groups use guns to carry out violent offenses covered by hate crime statutes. Treasury bureaus work to intercept gun shipments into the U.S. and to regulate the illegal sale and possession of firearms by potential perpetrators of hate crimes and other offenses.

Prosecuting Hate Crimes Aimed at Our Houses of Worship

Fighting Hate Crimes Aimed at Houses of Worship. The President fought for and signed the Church Arson Prevention Act of 1996, which facilitates prosecutions of racially motivated arsons and other acts of desecration against houses of worship.

Creating the National Church Arson Task Force. President Clinton established the National Church Arson Task Force (NCATF) in June 1996 to oversee the investigation and prosecution of arsons at houses of worship around the country. The NCATF has brought together the FBI, ATF, and Justice Department prosecutors in partnership with state and local law enforcement officers and prosecutors. Well over 200 ATF and FBI investigators have been deployed in these investigations. In addition, the NCATF has coordinated with other agencies, such as the Federal Emergency Management Agency and the Department of Housing and Urban Development, in the federal government's efforts to promote arson prevention and provide resources for church rebuilding.

Many of the 508 incidents investigated by NCATF have been solved, mainly by a combination of federal and state arrests and prosecutions. Since January 1995, there have been 240 arrests and over 100 convictions, including the first convictions under the Church Arson Prevention Act. This rate of arrest (35 percent) for crimes that may have been motivated by hate or bias is more than double the 16 percent rate of arrest for arsons in general.

Working with Communities Against Hate

Bringing Communities Together to Fight Hate. The Department of Justice's Community Relations Service often becomes involved when a hate crime incident threatens harmonious racial and ethnic relations in a community. The Service uses mediation to provide representatives of community groups and local governments with an impartial forum to restore stability through dialogue and discussion. It conducts training conferences on how to prevent and respond to hate crimes for state and local law enforcement and agencies, academic institutions, and civic, business, and community organizations.

Focusing on Youth Attitudes that Create Hate Crimes. The Department of Education is supporting efforts at the local level to develop and implement innovative and effective strategies for preventing hate crimes, including by funding programs aimed at reducing violent, hate-motivated behavior among youth.

Understanding the Problem of Hate Crimes

Gathering Information on the National Scope of the Problem. The FBI Uniform Crime Report collects the only national data on hate crimes through the Uniform Crime Reporting (UCR) Program. In 1996, 11,355 law enforcement agencies, representing 84 percent of the nation's population, participated in the FBI's data collection efforts. These departments reported 8,759 incidents of hate crimes in 1996.

Studying Hate Crimes

The National Institute of Mental Health (NIMH) has funded the first large-scale study of the mental health consequences of hate crimes, focusing on anti-gay hate crimes. The preliminary findings of this research are that hate crimes have more serious psychological effects on victims than do non-bias motivated, but otherwise similar crimes. The study also provides information about the prevalence of anti-gay hate crimes and the rate at which these crimes are reported to the police.

National Church Arson Task Force
First Year Report for the President

Established by President Clinton in June 1996, this governmental task force investigated church arsons throughout the country from January 1, 1995, through May 27, 1997. The following excerpts document the task force's goals, accomplishments, and conclusions regarding church arson hate crimes.

Overview

In early 1996, federal officials detected a sharp rise in the number of reported attacks on our nation's houses of worship, especially African American churches in the South. This trend troubled communities, challenged law enforcement agencies, and stirred the nation's conscience.

In June 1996, President Clinton formed the National Church Arson Task Force ("NCATF" or "Task Force"), made the investigation of these fires a top priority of federal law enforcement, and called on all Americans to come together in a spirit of respect and reconciliation.

The President directed his Administration to implement a strategy to (1) identify and prosecute the arsonists; (2) help communities rebuild the burned houses of worship; and (3) offer assistance in preventing more fires. Working with state and local law enforcement and private groups, federal officials achieved great success on these fronts. Significantly, many Americans came together as a result of these arsons, often independent of the federal effort, to lend assistance in many ways.

Prosecutions

- 429 Investigations Launched—The NCATF has opened 429 investigations into arsons, bombings or attempted bombings that have occurred at houses of worship between January 1, 1995, and May 27, 1997.
- 199 Arrested—Federal, state and local authorities have arrested 199 suspects since January 1995, in connection with 150 of the 429 investigations.
- 35 percent Solved—The 35 percent rate of arrest in NCATF cases is more than double the 16 percent rate of arrest for arsons in general.
- 110 Convicted—Federal and state prosecutors have successfully convicted 110 individuals in connection with fires at 77 houses of worship.

Rebuilding

- The Department of Housing and Urban Development (HUD) is working closely with the National Council of Churches, the Congress of National Black Churches, Habitat for Humanity and other organizations in the rebuilding effort.

• As a result of this cooperation, 25 houses of worship have been rebuilt and 65 are undergoing construction.

• HUD is administering a $10 million Federal Loan Guarantee Fund—established by Congress as part of the 1996 Church Arson Prevention Act—to assist with the rebuilding effort.

Prevention

• Arson prevention efforts continue across the nation. The U.S. Department of Justice awarded $3 million in grants to counties in 13 states to intensify their enforcement and surveillance efforts around vulnerable houses of worship, and the Federal Emergency Management Agency (FEMA) awarded approximately $1.5 million in arson prevention and training grants.

• FEMA established a Clearinghouse for arson prevention resources that has received over 15,000 telephone inquiries from all 50 states and the District of Columbia.

• FEMA has distributed more than 500,000 arson prevention packets, including the NCATF Church Threat Assessment Guide.

• FEMA efforts also include a four-city pilot project in Nashville, TN, Charlotte, NC, Macon, GA, and Utica, NY, to develop grass-roots arson prevention programs.

Led by James E. Johnson, Assistant Secretary of the Treasury for Enforcement, and Isabelle Katz Pinzler, Acting Assistant Attorney General for Civil Rights, who replaced Deval L. Patrick, former Assistant Attorney General, the NCATF formalized the coordination of investigations already underway. The NCATF brought together the Bureau of Alcohol, Tobacco and Firearms (ATF), the Federal Bureau of Investigation (FBI), Justice Department prosecutors, United States Attorneys, victim/witness coordinators, the Community Relations Service (CRS) and the U.S. Marshals Service, in partnership with state and local officers and prosecutors.

The efforts of the NCATF have been aided significantly by support from Congress, which provided additional statutory authority and resources for these investigations.

Reconciliations

Reaching Out to the Affected Communities

Without the confidence and cooperation of the congregations whose houses of worship burned, many of these investigations, which were difficult at the outset, would have been destined to fail. Faced with criticism of law enforcement from some congregations, the NCATF took steps early on to ensure solid, working relationships between law enforcement and the affected communities.

Less than a week after being formalized, the NCATF met with FBI and ATF Special Agents in Charge and U.S. Attorneys from the Southeast region to discuss the perceptions within the affected communities and to emphasize the critical importance of pursuing the investigations with vigilance, determination and dispatch, as well as with sensitivity to the needs of the victims. Following these meetings, the agents and prosecutors, together with representatives from the CRS, worked to improve lines of communications with the affected communities and make their commitment to these investigations clear.

President Clinton, Vice President Gore, Secretary of the Treasury Robert Rubin and Attorney General Reno have helped reach out to the affected communities, by bringing the church arsons to the nation's attention, speaking out forcefully on the commitment of the federal government to solve these arsons and meeting with ministers from the burned churches.

In June 1996, President Clinton traveled to the site of a burned African American church in Greeleyville, SC, to help dedicate a new church. Later that month, he organized an interfaith breakfast where he called on leaders of all faiths to open discussions to resolve our nation's racial and religious divisions. In August, the President and Vice President and their families traveled to Fruitland, TN, to help rebuild a church that had been destroyed earlier.

The President also convened a meeting of governors from affected states, who have worked hard to marshal resources in their states to help investigate arsons, prevent future arsons, and rebuild burned houses of worship. He also acknowledged the work of many groups which responded to these incidents, including the National Council of Churches, the Anti-Defamation League, the Southern Christian Leadership Conference, the National Association of Evangelicals, and the NAACP.

In addition to meeting with representatives from these groups and the Congressional Black Caucus, Assistant Secretary Johnson, then-Assistant Attorney General Patrick, and current Acting Assistant Attorney General Pinzler, have visited churches in the South to reinforce the Task Force's commitment to these investigations and view the devastation these arsons have wrought.

Dispatching Conflict Resolution Experts

The Community Relations Service (CRS) also has been an important partner in Task Force outreach efforts. Conflict resolution experts from CRS have worked in many communities across the country to identify and resolve racial conflicts and reduce racial tensions, to foster healthy relationships between law enforcement and minority communities and to facilitate communications among all parties.

The NCATF also developed, with the help of CRS, a "Best Practices" guide for conducting community outreach activities.

CRS plays an integral part in the Administration's response in local towns and cities, working with over 150 local communities in reducing racial polarization, bridging communication between law enforcement and minority communities, facilitating a biracial rebuilding effort, and training law enforcement on cultural diversity and race relations. Throughout the South, CRS convened a series of dialogues on race relations in an effort to reduce the likelihood of further church burnings.

Watching the Nation Respond

In addition to the efforts of Congress, federal agencies and the states, many private companies and organizations, as well as an untold number of Americans, pitched in to respond to the arsons.

Private companies offered funds and materials to help rebuild the burned churches. Transportation companies offered reduced fares for volunteers who traveled south to lend a hand.

And thousands of Americans donated time and money to support these efforts. Habitat for Humanity estimates that more than 15,000 individuals volunteered to help in the rebuilding process.

Seventy-three VISTA and AmeriCorps volunteers traveled to 18 rural communities in which church arsons have occurred and to over 70 other communities in Alabama, Georgia, Louisiana, Mississippi, North Carolina, South Carolina and Tennessee. In these communities, volunteers conducted community and church threat assessments, organized arson watch groups and town hall meetings on arson prevention, and engaged in community relations projects.

In the end, Americans of all walks of life refused to let these acts of destruction tear apart our communities or our nation.

Drawing Preliminary Conclusions

Although the investigations of most of the fires continue, the charges filed and the convictions obtained to date enable the Task Force to offer some preliminary conclusions. These conclusions are not based on cases sufficient to support additional charges. As a result, the Task Force cannot answer all of the questions raised by the fires.

Damage

Hundreds of houses of worship burned, congregations were temporarily displaced, and many people were left wondering how this could happen in the 1990's. These arsons destroyed rural wooden churches, ruined 100-year-old Bibles, and caused tens of millions of dollars in damage. But those communities which suffered a burned house of worship came to realize that thousands of Americans really care. The arsonists may have sought to divide our communities by burning our houses of worship, but in the end they only helped bring them closer together.

Multiple Motives

The arsons at African American churches raised significant fears about an increase in racially motivated crimes. As a result of our efforts to date, we have determined that the arsons—at both African American and other houses of worship—were motivated by a wide array of factors, including not only blatant racism or religious hatred, but also financial profit, burglary, and personal revenge. The Task Force continues to investigate many cases. When sufficient evidence of racial motive is developed, we will continue to seek and obtain criminal civil rights convictions, as we have against 14 of the 25 defendants convicted of federal charges in Alabama, Nevada, North Carolina, South Carolina, Tennessee and Texas.

National Conspiracy

While the Task Force continues to explore the question whether there are connections between the fires across the nation, the cases closed to date and the charges that have been filed do not support the theory that these fires were the product of a nationwide conspiracy. For instance, the Task Force has found that only a few of the fires are linked by common defendants. Conspiracy charges have been filed in a limited number of cases. These conspiracies, though, have tended to be confined to the small geographic areas where the arsons have occurred.

Hate Group Involvement

While there have been a handful of cases in which members and former members of hate groups, such as the Ku Klux Klan, have been convicted for arsons at houses of worship, most of the defendants were not found to be members of hate groups. Prosecutors need not show, however, that a defendant belongs to a particular hate group in order to gain a conviction.

Investigations Continue

The Task Force continues to investigate and prosecute those responsible for burning our nation's houses of worship. It is, therefore, too soon for the task force to speak conclusively about the motivation behind many of the fires at churches and other houses of worship. While it was the number of fires at African American churches that brought these crimes to national attention, the NCATF will continue to investigate and prosecute attacks on all houses of worship, regardless of their denomination or racial composition.

Expressing Sense of Congress with Respect to Recent Church Burnings

The terrible wave of church bombings from 1995 through 1997 evoked strong emotion throughout the United States. The following resolutions, introduced by Senator Carol Moseley-Braun (D-IL), the only African-American Senator, and Congressman J. C. Watt (R-OK), an African-American Representative, were approved unanimously by the Senate and House of Representatives.

(House of Representatives—June 13, 1996)
H. Con. Res. 187
Whereas more than 30 African-American churches have been burned over the last 18 months;
Whereas arrests have been made in only 5 of the cases currently under investigation;
Whereas the African-American community deserves the full support of Congress in solving these cases in an expeditious manner and it is important for Congress to speak out against the recent incidents of arson; and

Whereas several measures which would expedite the investigation into these incidents and assist in the prosecution of individuals found guilty of involvement in these incidents are now pending before Congress:

Now, therefore, be it resolved by the House of Representatives (the Senate concurring), that it is the sense of Congress that—

(1) attacks on places of worship because of the race, color, denomination, or ethnicity of the congregation undermine fundamental American ideals;

(2) these fires appear to be hate crimes and also implicitly interfere with the First Amendment rights and other civil rights of the victims;

(3) the arson of a place of worship is repulsive to us as a society;

(4) the Congress condemns, in the strongest possible terms, these abhorrent actions against freely worshipping American citizens and the African-American community in particular;

(5) the Congress sends its sincere condolences to those individuals who have been affected by these acts of cowardice;

(6) the Congress fully supports the activities of local law enforcement officials, the Department of Justice, and the Department of the Treasury in investigating these incidents;

(7) the Congress urges the United States Attorney General and local prosecutors to seek the maximum penalty available under law to punish the perpetrators of these craven acts;

(8) it is important that Congress enact appropriate legislation to ensure that Federal law enforcement has the necessary tools to punish and deter these shameful, vile acts, including the bipartisan legislation introduced by Representatives Hyde and Conyers which would facilitate the prosecution of persons responsible for these acts;

(9) the President is urged to make the fullest possible use of all available law enforcement resources to bring the culprits in these crimes to justice;

(10) Congress encourages the people of the United States to work within their own communities to prevent arson against African-American or any other house of worship; and

(11) Congress encourages American citizens to observe a national week of prayer beginning June 16, 1996, and ending June 23, 1996, in their churches, synagogues, mosques, and other places of worship for racial harmony, religious

tolerance and respect for the civil and human rights of all Americans.

Passed the House of Representatives June 13, 1996.

Hate Crimes Prevention Act of 1998 (S 1529 IS)

As this volume went to press, the U.S. Congress avoided considering additional legislation to curb hate-motivated violence in the country. Originally introduced in both the Senate and the House of Representatives in November 1997, the Hate Crimes Prevention Act of 1998 enhances the powers of the federal government to prosecute the perpetrators of violent hate crimes. In July 1998, the U.S. House of Representatives Subcommittee on Crime and also the U.S. Senate Committee on the Judiciary held hearings on this legislation, but Congress adjourned in October 1998 without debating the legislation.

The following documents include the text of the bill proposed in the Senate (S. 1529), which was identical to the House of Representatives bill (H.R. 3081). The House bill was introduced by Representatives Schumer (D-NY) and McCollum (R-FL) with more than 100 cosponsors; the Senate bill was introduced by Senators Kennedy (D-MA), Specter (R-PA), Wyden (D-OR), Feinstein (D-CA), and Torricelli (D-NJ).

This chapter also contains the text of the statement issued by the Anti-Defamation League before the House Judiciary Committee on July 22, 1998, in support of the Hate Crimes Prevention Act. It provides a concise summary of the purpose and need for this new legislation.

To enhance Federal enforcement of hate crimes, and for other purposes.

November 13, 1997

Be it enacted by the Senate and House of Representatives of the United States of America in Congress assembled,

Section 1. Short Title.

This Act may be cited as the 'Hate Crimes Prevention Act of 1998'.

Sec. 2. Findings.

Congress finds that—

(1) the incidence of violence motivated by the actual or perceived race, color, national origin, religion, sexual

orientation, gender, or disability of the victim poses a serious national problem;

(2) such violence disrupts the tranquility and safety of communities and is deeply divisive;

(3) existing Federal law is inadequate to address this problem;

(4) such violence affects interstate commerce in many ways, including—

(A) by impeding the movement of members of targeted groups and forcing such members to move across State lines to escape the incidence or risk of such violence; and

(B) by preventing members of targeted groups from purchasing goods and services, obtaining or sustaining employment or participating in other commercial activity;

(5) perpetrators cross State lines to commit such violence;

(6) instrumentalities of interstate commerce are used to facilitate the commission of such violence;

(7) such violence is committed using articles that have traveled in interstate commerce;

(8) violence motivated by bias that is a relic of slavery can constitute badges and incidents of slavery;

(9) although many local jurisdictions have attempted to respond to the challenges posed by such violence, the problem is sufficiently serious, widespread, and interstate in scope to warrant Federal intervention to assist such jurisdictions; and

(10) many States have no laws addressing violence based on the actual or perceived race, color, national origin, religion, sexual orientation, gender, or disability of the victim, while other States have laws that provide only limited protection.

Sec. 3. Definition of Hate Crime.

In this Act, the term 'hate crime' has the same meaning as in section 280003(a) of the Violent Crime Control and Law Enforcement Act of 1994 (28 U.S.C. 994 note).

Sec. 4. Prohibition of Certain Acts of Violence.

Section 245 of title 18, United States Code, is amended—

(1) by redesignating subsections (c) and (d) as subsections (d) and (e), respectively; and

(2) by inserting after subsection (b) the following:

(c)(1) Whoever, whether or not acting under color of law, willfully causes bodily injury to any person or, through the use of fire, a firearm, or an explosive device, attempts to cause bodily injury to any person, because of the actual or perceived race, color, religion, or national origin of any person—

(A) shall be imprisoned not more than 10 years, or fined in accordance with this title, or both; and

(B) shall be imprisoned for any term of years or for life, or fined in accordance with this title, or both if—

(i) death results from the acts committed in violation of this paragraph; or

(ii) the acts committed in violation of this paragraph include kidnapping or an attempt to kidnap, aggravated sexual abuse or an attempt to commit aggravated sexual abuse, or an attempt to kill.

(2)(A) Whoever, whether or not acting under color of law, in any circumstance described in subparagraph (B), willfully causes bodily injury to any person or, through the use of fire, a firearm, or an explosive device, attempts to cause bodily injury to any person, because of the actual or perceived religion, gender, sexual orientation, or disability of any person—

(i) shall be imprisoned not more than 10 years, or fined in accordance with this title, or both; and

(ii) shall be imprisoned for any term of years or for life, or fined in accordance with this title, or both, if—

(I) death results from the acts committed in violation of this paragraph; or

(II) the acts committed in violation of this paragraph include kidnapping or an attempt to kidnap, aggravated sexual abuse or an attempt to commit aggravated sexual abuse, or an attempt to kill.

(B) For purposes of subparagraph (A), the circumstances described in this subparagraph are that—

(i) in connection with the offense, the defendant or the victim travels in interstate or foreign commerce, uses a facility or instrumentality of interstate or foreign commerce, or engages in any activity affecting interstate or foreign commerce; or

(ii) the offense is in or affects interstate or foreign commerce.

Sec. 5. Duties of Federal Sentencing Commission.

(a) Amendment of Federal Sentencing Guidelines—
Pursuant to its authority under section 994 of title 28, United States Code, the United States Sentencing Commission

shall study the issue of adult recruitment of juveniles to commit hate crimes and shall, if appropriate, amend the Federal sentencing guidelines to provide sentencing enhancements (in addition to the sentencing enhancement provided for the use of a minor during the commission of an offense) for adult defendants who recruit juveniles to assist in the commission of hate crimes.

(b) Consistency with Other Guidelines—In carrying out this section, the United States Sentencing Commission shall—

(1) ensure that there is reasonable consistency with other Federal sentencing guidelines; and

(2) avoid duplicative punishments for substantially the same offense.

Sec. 6. Grant Program.

(a) Authority to Make Grants—The Administrator of the Office of Juvenile Justice and Delinquency Prevention of the Department of Justice shall make grants, in accordance with such regulations as the Attorney General may prescribe, to State and local programs designed to combat hate crimes committed by juveniles.

(b) Authorization of Appropriations—There are authorized to be appropriated such sums as may be necessary to carry out this section.

Sec. 7. Authorization for Additional Personnel to Assist State and Local Law Enforcement.

There are authorized to be appropriated to the Department of the Treasury and the Department of Justice, including the Community Relations Service, for fiscal years 1998, 1999, and 2000 such sums as are necessary to increase the number of personnel to prevent and respond to alleged violations of section 245 of title 18, United States Code (as amended by this Act).

Sec. 8. Severability.

If any provision of this Act, an amendment made by this Act, or the application of such provision or amendment to any person or circumstance is held to be unconstitutional, the remainder of this Act, the amendments made by this Act, and the application of the provisions of such to any person or circumstance shall not be affected thereby.

Wisconsin v. Mitchell, 508 U.S. 476 (1993)

In June 1993, the United States Supreme Court upheld a Wisconsin statute that provides for an enhanced sentence when the defendant "intentionally selects a person against whom a crime is committed because of the race, religion, color, disability, sexual orientation, national origin, or ancestry of that person." The Court also made clear that the "First Amendment . . . does not prohibit the evidentiary use of speech to establish the elements of a crime or to prove motive or intent." According to many legal scholars, this case, Wisconsin v. Mitchell, *appears to have foreclosed any serious challenges to penalty enhancement statutes on the basis of the First Amendment to the Constitution. The first opinion is from the Wisconsin State Court of Appeals, which held that hate crime statutes do not violate First Amendment rights; the second opinion is the affirmation of that decision by the U.S. Supreme Court.*

Wisconsin v. Mitchell Certiorari to the Supreme Court of Wisconsin, No. 92–515

Argued April 21, 1993

Decided June 11, 1993

Pursuant to a Wisconsin statute, respondent Mitchell's sentence for aggravated battery was enhanced because he intentionally selected his victim on account of the victim's race. The State Court of Appeals rejected his challenge to the law's constitutionality, but the State Supreme Court reversed. Relying on *R.A.V. v. St. Paul,* 505 U.S. 377, it held that the statute violates the First Amendment by punishing what the legislature has deemed to be offensive thought and rejected the State's contention that the law punishes only the conduct of intentional victim selection. It also found that the statute was unconstitutionally overbroad because the evidentiary use of a defendant's prior speech would have a chilling effect on those who fear they may be prosecuted for offenses subject to penalty enhancement. Finally, it distinguished antidiscrimination laws, which have long been held constitutional, on the ground that they prohibit objective acts of discrimination, whereas the state statute punishes the subjective mental process.

Held:

Mitchell's First Amendment rights were not violated by the application of the penalty-enhancement provision in sentencing him. Pp. 483–490.

(a) While Mitchell correctly notes that this Court is bound by a state court's interpretation of a state statute, the State Supreme Court did not construe the instant statute in the sense of defining the meaning of a particular word or phrase. Rather, it characterized the statute's practical effect for First Amendment purposes. Thus, after resolving any ambiguities in the statute's meaning, this Court may form its own judgment about the law's operative effect. The State's argument that the statute punishes only conduct does not dispose of Mitchell's claim, since the fact remains that the same criminal conduct is more heavily punished if the victim is selected because of his protected status than if no such motive obtains. Pp. 483–485.

(b) In determining what sentence to impose, sentencing judges have traditionally considered a wide variety of factors in addition to evidence bearing on guilt, including a defendant's motive for committing the offense. While it is equally true that a sentencing judge may not take into consideration a defendant's abstract beliefs, however obnoxious to most people, the Constitution does not erect a *per se* barrier to the admission of evidence concerning one's beliefs and associations at sentencing simply because they are protected by the First Amendment. *Dawson v. Delaware,* 503 U.S. 159; *Barclay v. Florida,* 463 U.S. 939 (plurality opinion). That *Dawson* and *Barclay* did not involve the application of a penalty-enhancement provision does not make them inapposite. *Barclay* involved the consideration of racial animus in determining whether to sentence a defendant to death, the most severe "enhancement" of all; and the state legislature has the primary responsibility for fixing criminal penalties. Motive plays the same role under the state statute as it does under federal and state antidiscrimination laws, which have been upheld against constitutional challenge. Nothing in *R.A.V. v. St. Paul*, supra, compels a different result here. The ordinance at issue there was explicitly directed at speech, while the one here is aimed at conduct unprotected by the First Amendment. Moreover, the State's desire to redress what it sees as the greater individual and societal harm inflicted by bias-inspired conduct provides an adequate explanation for the provision over and above mere disagreement with offenders' beliefs or biases. Pp. 485–488.

(c) Because the statute has no "chilling effect" on free speech, it is not unconstitutionally overbroad. The prospect of a citizen suppressing his bigoted beliefs for fear that evidence of those beliefs will be introduced against him at trial if he commits a serious offense against person or property is too speculative a hypothesis to support this claim. Moreover, the First Amendment permits the admission of previous

declarations or statements to establish the elements of a crime
or to prove motive or intent, subject to evidentiary rules dealing
with relevancy, reliability, and the like. *Haupt v. United States,*
330 U.S. 631. Pp. 488–490.

169 Wis.2d 153, 485 N.W.2d 807 (1992), reversed and
remanded.

Chief Justice Rehnquist delivered the following opinion of
the U.S. Supreme Court:

Respondent Todd Mitchell's sentence for aggravated
battery was enhanced because he intentionally selected his
victim on account of the victim's race. The question presented
in this case is whether this penalty enhancement is prohibited
by the First and Fourteenth Amendments. We hold that it is not.

On the evening of October 7, 1989, a group of young black
men and boys, including Mitchell, gathered at an apartment
[508 U.S. 476, 480] complex in Kenosha, Wisconsin. Several
members of the group discussed a scene from the motion
picture "Mississippi Burning" in which a white man beat a
young black boy who was praying. The group moved outside
and Mitchell asked them: "'Do you all feel hyped up to move
on some white people?'" Brief for Petitioner 4. Shortly
thereafter, a young white boy approached the group on the
opposite side of the street where they were standing. As the boy
walked by, Mitchell said: "'You all want to fuck somebody up?
There goes a white boy; go get him.'" Id. at 4–5. Mitchell
counted to three and pointed in the boy's direction. The group
ran toward the boy, beat him severely, and stole his tennis
shoes. The boy was rendered unconscious and remained in a
coma for four days.

After a jury trial in the Circuit Court for Kenosha County,
Mitchell was convicted of aggravated battery. Wis.Stat. 939.05
and 940.19(1m) (1989–1990). That offense ordinarily carries a
maximum sentence of two years' imprisonment. 940.19(1m) and
939.50(3)(e). But because the jury found that Mitchell had
intentionally selected his victim because of the boy's race, the
maximum sentence for Mitchell's offense was increased to
seven years under 939.645. That provision enhances the
maximum penalty for an offense whenever the defendant
"[i]ntentionally selects the person against whom the crime . . .
is committed . . . because of the race, religion, color, disability,
sexual orientation, national origin or ancestry of that
person. . . ." [508 U.S. 476, 481] 939.645(1)(b). The Circuit

Court sentenced Mitchell to four years' imprisonment for the aggravated battery.

Mitchell unsuccessfully sought postconviction relief in the Circuit Court. Then he appealed his conviction and sentence, challenging the constitutionality of Wisconsin's penalty-enhancement provision on First Amendment grounds. The Wisconsin Court of Appeals rejected Mitchell's challenge, 163 Wis.2d 652, 473 N.W.2d 1 (1991), but the Wisconsin Supreme Court reversed. The Supreme Court [508 U.S. 476, 482] held that the statute "violates the First Amendment directly by punishing what the legislature has deemed to be offensive thought." 169 Wis.2d 153, 163, 485 N.W.2d 807, 811 (1992). It rejected the State's contention "that the statute punishes only the 'conduct' of intentional selection of a victim." Id. at 164, 485 N.W.2d at 812. According to the court, "[t]he statute punishes the 'because of' aspect of the defendant's selection, the reason the defendant selected the victim, the motive behind the selection." Ibid. (emphasis in original). And under *R.A.V. v. St. Paul*, 505 U.S. 377 (1992), "the Wisconsin legislature cannot criminalize bigoted thought with which it disagrees." 169 Wis.2d at 171, 485 N.W.2d at 815.

The Supreme Court also held that the penalty-enhancement statute was unconstitutionally overbroad. It reasoned that, in order to prove that a defendant intentionally selected his victim because of the victim's protected status, the State would often have to introduce evidence of the defendant's prior speech, such as racial epithets he may have uttered before the commission of the offense. This evidentiary use of protected speech, the court thought, would have a "chilling effect" on those who feared the possibility of prosecution for offenses subject to penalty enhancement. See id. at 174, 485 N.W.2d at 816. Finally, the court distinguished antidiscrimination laws, which have long been held constitutional, on the ground that the Wisconsin statute punishes the "subjective mental process" of selecting a victim because of his protected status, whereas antidiscrimination laws prohibit "objective acts of discrimination." Id. at 176, 485 N.W.2d at 817.

We granted certiorari because of the importance of the question presented and the existence of a conflict of authority [508 U.S. 476, 483] among state high courts on the constitutionality of statutes similar to Wisconsin's penalty-enhancement provision, 506 U.S. 1033 (1992). We reverse.

Mitchell argues that we are bound by the Wisconsin

Supreme Court's conclusion that the statute punishes bigoted thought, and not conduct. There is no doubt that we are bound by a state court's construction of a state statute. *R. A. V.,* supra, at 381; *New York v. Ferber,* 458 U.S. 747, 769, n. 24 (1982); *Terminiello v. Chicago,* 337 U.S. 1, 4 (1949). In *Terminiello,* for example, the Illinois courts had defined the term "'breach of the peace,'" in a city ordinance prohibiting disorderly conduct, to include "'stirs the public to anger . . . or creates a disturbance.'" Id. at 4. We held this construction [508 U.S. 476, 484] to be binding on us. But here the Wisconsin Supreme Court did not, strictly speaking, construe the Wisconsin statute in the sense of defining the meaning of a particular statutory word or phrase. Rather, it merely characterized the "practical effect" of the statute for First Amendment purposes. See 169 Wis.2d at 166–167, 485 N.W.2d at 813 ("Merely because the statute refers in a literal sense to the intentional 'conduct' of selecting, does not mean the court must turn a blind eye to the intent and practical effect of the law—punishment of motive or thought"). This assessment does not bind us. Once any ambiguities as to the meaning of the statute are resolved, we may form our own judgment as to its operative effect.

The State argues that the statute does not punish bigoted thought, as the Supreme Court of Wisconsin said, but instead punishes only conduct. While this argument is literally correct, it does not dispose of Mitchell's First Amendment challenge. To be sure, our cases reject the "view that an apparently limitless variety of conduct can be labeled 'speech' whenever the person engaging in the conduct intends thereby to express an idea." *United States v. O'Brien,* 391 U.S. 367, 376 (1968); accord, *R. A. V.,* 505 U.S. at 385–386; *Spence v. Washington,* 418 U.S. 405, 409 (1974) (per curiam); *Cox v. Louisiana,* 379 U.S. 536, 555 (1965). Thus, a physical assault is not, by any stretch of the imagination, expressive conduct protected by the First Amendment. See *Roberts v. United States Jaycees,* 468 U.S. 609, 628 (1984) ("[V]iolence or other types of potentially expressive activities that produce special harms distinct from their communicative impact . . . are entitled to no constitutional protection"); *NAACP v. Claiborne Hardware Co.,* 458 U.S. 886, 916 (1982) ("The First Amendment does not protect violence").

But the fact remains that, under the Wisconsin statute, the same criminal conduct may be more heavily punished if the victim is selected because of his race or other protected status [508 U.S. 476, 485] than if no such motive obtained. Thus, although the statute punishes criminal conduct, it enhances the maximum penalty for conduct motivated by a discriminatory point of view more severely than the same conduct engaged in for some other reason or for no reason at all. Because the only reason for the enhancement is the defendant's discriminatory motive for selecting his victim, Mitchell argues (and the Wisconsin Supreme Court held) that the statute violates the First Amendment by punishing offenders' bigoted beliefs.

[Traditionally, sentencing judges have considered a wide variety of factors in addition to evidence bearing on guilt in determining what sentence to impose on a convicted defendant.] See *Payne v. Tennessee*, 501 U.S. 808 820–821 (1991); *United States v. Tucker*, 404 U.S. 443, 446 (1972); *Williams v. New York*, 337 U.S. 241, 246 (1949). The defendant's motive for committing the offense is one important factor. See 1 W. LeFave & A. Scott, *Substantive Criminal Law* 3.6(b), p. 324 (1986) ("Motives are most relevant when the trial judge sets the defendant's sentence, and it is not uncommon for a defendant to receive a minimum sentence because he was acting with good motives, or a rather high sentence because of his bad motives"); cf. *Tison v. Arizona*, 481 U.S. 137, 156 (1987) ("Deeply ingrained in our legal tradition is the idea that the more purposeful is the criminal conduct, the more serious is the offense, and, therefore, the more severely it ought to be punished"). Thus, in many States, the commission of a murder or other capital offense for pecuniary gain is a separate aggravating circumstance under the capital sentencing statute. See, e.g., Ariz.Rev.Stat.Ann. 13–703(F)(5) (1989); Fla.Stat. 921.141(5)(f) (Supp. 1992); Miss.Code Ann. 99–19–101(5)(f) (Supp. 1992); N.C.Gen.Stat. 15A-2000(e)(6) (1992); Wyo.Stat. 6–2–102(h)(vi) (Supp. 1992).

But it is equally true that a defendant's abstract beliefs, however obnoxious to most people, may not be taken into consideration by a sentencing judge. *Dawson v. Delaware,* [508 U.S. 476, 486] 503 U.S. 159 (1992). In *Dawson,* the State introduced evidence at a capital sentencing hearing that the defendant was a member of a white supremacist prison gang. Because "the evidence proved nothing more than [the defendant's] abstract beliefs," we held that its admission violated the defendant's First Amendment rights. Id. at 167. In so holding, however, we emphasized that "the Constitution does not erect a *per se* barrier to the admission of evidence concerning one's beliefs and associations at sentencing simply because those beliefs and associations are protected by the First Amendment." Id. at 165. Thus, in *Barclay v. Florida*, 463 U.S. 939 (1983) (plurality opinion), we allowed the sentencing judge to take into account the defendant's racial animus towards his victim. The evidence in that case showed that the defendant's membership in the Black Liberation Army and desire to provoke a "race war" were related to the murder of a white man for which he was convicted. See id. at 942–944. Because "the elements of racial hatred in [the] murder" were relevant to several aggravating factors, we held that the trial judge permissibly took this evidence into account in sentencing the defendant to death. Id. at 949, and n. 7.

Mitchell suggests that *Dawson* and *Barclay* are inapposite because they did not involve application of a penalty-enhancement provision. But in *Barclay* we held that it was permissible for the sentencing court to consider the defendant's racial animus in determining whether he should be sentenced to death, surely the most severe "enhancement" of all. And the fact that the Wisconsin Legislature has decided, as a general matter, that bias-motivated offenses warrant greater maximum penalties across the board does not alter the result here. For the primary responsibility for fixing criminal penalties lies with the legislature. *Rummel v. Estelle*, 445 U.S. 263, 274 (1980); *Gore v. United States*, 357 U.S. 386, 393 (1958). [508 U.S. 476, 487]

Mitchell argues that the Wisconsin penalty-enhancement statute is invalid because it punishes the defendant's discriminatory motive, or reason, for acting. But motive plays the same role under the Wisconsin statute as it does under federal and state antidiscrimination laws, which we have previously upheld against constitutional challenge. See *Roberts v. United States Jaycees*, supra, at 628; *Hishon v. King & Spalding*, 467 U.S. 69, 78 (1984); *Runyon v. McCrary*, 427 U.S. 160, 176 (1976). Title VII of the Civil Rights Act of 1964, for example, makes it unlawful for an employer to discriminate against an employee "because of such individual's race, color, religion, sex, or national origin." 42 U.S.C. 2000e–2(a)(1) (emphasis added). In *Hishon*, we rejected the argument that Title VII infringed employers' First Amendment rights. And more recently, in *R. A. V. v. St. Paul*, 505 U.S. at 389–390, we cited Title VII (as well as 18 U.S.C. 242 and 42 U.S.C. 1981 and 1982) as an example of a permissible content-neutral regulation of conduct.

Nothing in our decision last term in *R. A. V.* compels a different result here. That case involved a First Amendment challenge to a municipal ordinance prohibiting the use of "'fighting words' that insult, or provoke violence, 'on the basis of race, color, creed, religion or gender.'" 505 U.S. at 391 (quoting St. Paul Bias-Motivated Crime Ordinance, St. Paul, Minn., Legis.Code 292.02 (1990). Because the ordinance only proscribed a class of "fighting words" deemed particularly offensive by the city—i.e., those "that contain . . . messages of 'bias-motivated' hatred," 505 U.S. at 392, we held that it violated the rule against content-based discrimination. See id. at 392–394. But whereas the ordinance struck down in *R. A. V.* was explicitly directed at expression (i.e., "speech" or "messages," id. at 392, the statute in this case is aimed at conduct unprotected by the First Amendment.

Moreover, the Wisconsin statute singles out for enhancement bias-inspired conduct because this conduct is thought [508 U.S. 476, 488] to inflict greater individual and societal harm. For example, according to the State and its amici, bias-motivated crimes are more likely to provoke retaliatory crimes, inflict distinct emotional harms on their victims, and incite community unrest. See, e.g., Brief for Petitioner 24–27; Brief for United States as Amicus Curiae 13–15; Brief for Lawyers' Committee for Civil Rights Under Law as Amicus Curiae 18–22; Brief for the American Civil Liberties Union as Amicus Curiae 17–19; Brief for the Anti-Defamation League et al. as Amici Curiae 910; Brief for Congressman Charles E. Schumer et al. as Amici Curiae 8–9. The State's desire to redress these perceived harms provides an adequate explanation for its penalty-enhancement provision over and above mere disagreement with offenders' beliefs or biases. As Blackstone said long ago, "it is but reasonable that, among crimes of different natures, those should be most severely punished which are the most destructive of the public safety and happiness." 4 W. Blackstone, Commentaries 16.

Finally, there remains to be considered Mitchell's argument that the Wisconsin statute is unconstitutionally overbroad because of its "chilling effect" on free speech. Mitchell argues (and the Wisconsin Supreme Court agreed) that the statute is "overbroad" because evidence of the defendant's prior speech or associations may be used to prove that the defendant intentionally selected his victim on account of the victim's protected status. Consequently, the argument goes, the statute impermissibly chills free expression with respect to such matters by those concerned about the possibility of enhanced sentences if they should, in the future, commit a criminal offense covered by the statute. We find no merit in this contention.

The sort of chill envisioned here is far more attenuated and unlikely than that contemplated in traditional "overbreadth" cases. We must conjure up a vision of a Wisconsin citizen suppressing his unpopular bigoted opinions for fear that, if he later commits an offense covered by the statute [508 U.S. 476, 489], these opinions will be offered at trial to establish that he selected his victim on account of the victim's protected status, thus qualifying him for penalty-enhancement. To stay within the realm of rationality, we must surely put to one side minor misdemeanor offenses covered by the statute, such as negligent operation of a motor vehicle [Wis.Stat. 941.01 (1989–1990)], for it is difficult, if not impossible, to conceive of a situation where such offenses would be racially motivated. We are left, then, with the prospect of a citizen suppressing his bigoted beliefs for fear that evidence of such beliefs will be introduced against him at trial if he commits a more serious offense against person or property. This is simply too speculative a hypothesis to support Mitchell's overbreadth claim.

The First Amendment, moreover, does not prohibit the evidentiary use of speech to establish the elements of a crime or to prove motive or intent. Evidence of a defendant's previous declarations or statements is commonly admitted in criminal trials subject to evidentiary rules dealing with relevancy, reliability, and the like. Nearly half a century ago, in *Haupt v. United States*, 330 U.S. 631 (1947), we rejected a contention similar to that advanced by Mitchell here. Haupt was tried for the offense of treason, which, as defined by the Constitution (Art. III, 3), may depend very much on proof of motive. To prove that the acts in question were committed out of "adherence to the enemy" rather than "parental solicitude," id. at 641, the Government introduced evidence of conversations that had taken place long prior to the indictment, some of which consisted of statements showing Haupt's sympathy with Germany and Hitler and hostility towards the United States. We rejected Haupt's argument that this evidence was improperly admitted. While "[s]uch testimony is to be scrutinized with care to be certain the statements are not expressions of mere lawful and permissible difference of opinion with our own government or quite proper appreciation of the land of birth, we held that "these statements . . . [508 U.S. 476, 490] clearly were admissible on the question of intent and adherence to the enemy." Id. at 642. See also *Price Waterhouse v. Hopkins,* 490 U.S. 228, 251–252 (1989) (plurality opinion) (allowing evidentiary use of defendant's speech in evaluating Title VII discrimination claim); *Street v. New York,* 394 U.S. 576, 594 (1969).

For the foregoing reasons, we hold that Mitchell's First Amendment rights were not violated by the application of the Wisconsin penalty-enhancement provision in sentencing him. The judgment of the Supreme Court of Wisconsin is therefore reversed, and the case is remanded for further proceedings not inconsistent with this opinion.

It is so ordered.

Nongovernment Documents

Statement of the Anti-Defamation League on the Hate Crimes Prevention Act (H.R. 3081), July 22, 1998

The Anti-Defamation League is pleased to provide testimony as the House Judiciary Committee conducts hearings on H.R. 3081, the Hate Crimes Prevention Act (HCPA). This necessary legislation, introduced under the leadership of Reps. Schumer and McCollum, would eliminate gaps in federal authority to investigate and prosecute bias-motivated crimes. Federal authorities must have jurisdiction to address those cases in which local authorities are either unable or unwilling to act.

Last month the nation was shocked by the senseless, brutal murder of James Byrd, Jr. in Jasper, Texas. Everything we know about this horrible crime indicates that Mr. Byrd was targeted for violence because of his race—allegedly by individuals associated with a white supremacist group. In this case, local law enforcement officials have responded effectively, but crimes of this magnitude transcend local communities and have national impact. To underscore the nation's determination to confront bias-motivated crimes, the federal government must have the opportunity to act in partnership with state and local officials. Where appropriate, the federal government should have the authority to take the lead in prosecuting these cases.

Under current federal law, the government must prove that the crime occurred because of a person's membership in a protected group, such as race or religion, *and because* he/she was engaging in a federally-protected activity (such as voting, going to school, or working). The HCPA would eliminate these overly-restrictive limitations and provide authority for federal investigations and prosecutions in cases in which the bias violence occurs because of the victim's sexual orientation, gender, or disability.

The Anti-Defamation League

Since 1913, the mission of ADL has been to "stop the defamation of the Jewish people and to secure justice and fair treatment to all citizens alike." Dedicated to combatting anti-Semitism, prejudice, and bigotry of all kinds, defending democratic ideals and promoting civil rights, ADL is proud of its leadership role in the development of innovative materials, programs, and services that build bridges of communication, understanding, and respect among diverse racial, religious, and ethnic groups.

Over the past decade, the League has been recognized as a leading resource on effective responses to violent bigotry, conducting an annual Audit of Anti-Semitic Incidents, drafting model hate crime statutes for state legislatures, and serving as a principal resource for the FBI in developing training and outreach materials for the Hate Crime Statistics Act (HCSA), which requires the Justice Department to collect statistics on hate violence from law enforcement officials across the country.

The attempt to eliminate prejudice requires that Americans develop respect and acceptance of cultural differences and begin to establish dialogue across ethnic, cultural, and religious boundaries. Education and exposure are the cornerstones of a long-term solution to prejudice, discrimination, bigotry, and anti-Semitism. Effective response to hate violence by public officials and law enforcement authorities can play an essential role in deterring and preventing these crimes.

Defining the Issue: The Impact of Hate Violence

All Americans have a stake in effective response to violent bigotry. These crimes demand a priority response because of their special impact on the victim and the victim's community. Bias crimes are designed to intimidate the victim and members of the victim's community, leaving them feeling isolated, vulnerable, and unprotected by the law. Failure to address this unique type of crime could cause an isolated incident to explode into widespread community tension. The damage done by hate crimes cannot be measured solely in terms of physical injury or dollars and cents. By making members of minority communities fearful, angry, and suspicious of other groups—and of the power structure that is supposed to protect them—these incidents can damage the fabric of our society and fragment communities.

Hate Crime Statutes: A Message to Victims and Perpetrators

In partnership with human rights groups, civic leaders and law enforcement officials can advance police-community relations by demonstrating a commitment to be both tough on hate crime perpetrators and sensitive to the special needs of hate crime victims. While bigotry cannot be outlawed, hate crime penalty enhancement statutes demonstrate an important commitment to confront criminal activity motivated by prejudice.

At present, forty states and the District of Columbia have enacted hate crime penalty-enhancement laws, many based on an ADL model statute drafted in 1981. In *Wisconsin v. Mitchell*, 508 U.S. 476 (1993), the U.S. Supreme Court unanimously upheld the constitutionality of the Wisconsin penalty-enhancement statute—effectively removing any doubt that state legislatures may properly increase the penalties for criminal activity in which the victim is intentionally targeted because of his/her race, religion, sexual orientation, gender, or ethnicity.

Improving the Federal Government's Response to Bias-Motivated Violence

The historic White House Conference on Hate Crimes on November 10, 1997 went far beyond the usual photo opportunities and Presidential pomp. Following the President's announcement of the Conference in an eloquent June 7 radio address on hate violence, Justice Department and Department of Education officials prepared comprehensive inventories of existing federal resources and programs on the issue. Working groups met repeatedly within the Justice Department, bringing together government experts, law enforcement groups, academics, and civil rights activists to assess future needs and establish priorities.

In speeches, panels, and workshops throughout the Conference, the President, the Vice President, and six Cabinet members stressed the importance of direct action against bias-motivated crime. The Conference itself provided the forum for the announcement of a number of substantive policy pronouncements, including: the establishment of regional U.S. Attorney-led police-community hate crime task forces, additional FBI hate crime investigators and Justice Department prosecutors, a Justice Department hate crime web site for children, the development of coordinated federal law enforcement hate crime training programs, a joint Justice Department/Education Department hate crime resource guide for public schools—and support for the HCPA.

Addressing Limitations in Existing Federal Civil Rights Statutes

The HCPA would amend Section 245 of Title 18 U.S.C., one of the primary statutes used to combat racial and religious bias-motivated violence. The current statute, enacted in 1968, prohibits intentional interference, by force or threat of force, with the enjoyment of a federal right or benefit (such as voting, going to school, or working) on the basis of race, color, religion, or national origin.

As mentioned, under the current statute, the government must prove *both* that the crime occurred because of a person's membership in a protected group, such as race or religion, *and because* (not *while*) he/she was engaging in a federally-protected activity. Justice Department officials have identified a number of significant racial violence cases in which federal prosecutions have been stymied by these unwieldy dual jurisdictional requirements. In addition, federal authorities are currently unable to involve themselves in cases involving death or serious bodily injury resulting from crimes directed at individuals because of their sexual orientation, gender, or disability—even when local law enforcement remedies are not available.

The HCPA would amend 18 U.S.C. 245 in two ways. First, the legislation would remove the overly-restrictive obstacles to federal involvement by permitting prosecutions without having to prove that the victim was attacked because he/she was engaged in a federally-protected activity. Second, it would provide new authority for federal officials to investigate and prosecute cases in which the bias violence occurs because of the victim's real or perceived sexual orientation, gender, or disability.

If adopted, the HCPA would expand the universe of possible federal criminal civil rights violations—and Congress and the Administration should match this increased authority with additional appropriations for FBI investigators and Justice Department prosecutors. Similarly, after expanding federal authority to address the disturbing series of attacks against houses of worship in the Church Arson Prevention Act of 1996, Congress provided additional funds to ensure that federal authorities had the resources to follow through on the promise of the new law.

Clearly, however, neither the sponsors nor the supporters of this measure expect that federal prosecutors will seek to investigate and prosecute every bias crime as a federal criminal civil rights violation. The vast majority of bias-motivated crimes should be handled by state and local law enforcement officials. But some crimes will merit federal involvement—for exactly the same reasons that Congress in 1968 determined that certain crimes directed at individuals because of "race, color, religion or national origin" required a federal remedy.

While recognizing that state and local law enforcement officials play the primary role in the prosecution of hate violence, the federal government must have clear authority to address those cases in which local officials are either unable or unwilling to investigate and prosecute. In those states without hate crime statutes, and in others with limited coverage, local prosecutors are simply not able to pursue bias crime convictions. Currently, only twenty-one states include sexual orientation-based crimes in their hate crimes statutes, twenty states include coverage of gender-based crimes, and twenty-two states include coverage for disability-based crimes. . . . Other cases which could clearly merit federal involvement include those in which local law enforcement officials refuse to act because, for example, the rapist or the batterer in a small town is a friend or relative of the Police Chief, the District Attorney, or the Mayor.

Limitations on Federal Hate Crime Prosecutions

As drafted, the HCPA contains a number of significant limitations on prosecutorial discretion. First, the bill's requirement of actual injury, or, in the case of crimes involving "the use of fire, a firearm, or any explosive device, an attempt to cause bodily injury," limits the federal government's jurisdiction to the most serious crimes of violence against individuals—not property crimes.

Second, for the proposed new categories—gender, sexual orientation, and disability—federal prosecutors will have to prove an interstate commerce connection with the crime— similar to the constitutional basis relied upon for the Church Arson Prevention Act passed unanimously by Congress in 1997.

Third, the HCPA retains the current certification requirement under 18 U.S.C. 245. This institutional limitation on prosecutions requires the Attorney General, or her/his designee, to certify in writing that an individual prosecution "is in the public interest and necessary to secure substantial justice."

Finally, Justice Department officials have traditionally been extremely selective in prosecuting cases under the federal criminal civil rights statutes. For example, in 1996, a year in which the FBI's HCSA report documented 8,759 crimes reported by 11,355 police agencies, the Justice Department brought only thirty-eight racial violence cases under *all* federal criminal civil rights statutes combined—and only eight cases under 18 U.S.C. 245. In fact, since its enactment in 1968, there have never been more than ten prosecutions per year under 18 U.S.C. 245. Federal prosecutors can be expected to continue to defer to state authorities under its expanded authority—but the HCPA will permit prosecutions of bias-motivated violence that might not otherwise receive the attention they deserve.

Supporters of the HCPA know well that new federal criminal civil rights jurisdiction to address crimes directed at individuals because of their gender, sexual orientation, or disability will not result in the elimination of these crimes. But the possibility of federal involvement in select cases, the impact of FBI investigations in others, and partnership arrangements with state and local investigators in still other cases, should prompt more effective state and local prosecutions of these crimes.

Recent Federal Responses to Hate Violence

The federal government has an essential leadership role to play in confronting criminal activity motivated by prejudice and in promoting prejudice reduction initiatives for schools and the community. In recent years, Congress has provided broad, bipartisan support for several federal initiatives to address these crimes. These initiatives have led to significant improvements in the response of the criminal justice system to bias-motivated crime. The HCPA is based on the hate crime definitions established in these previous enactments—and builds on the foundation of these existing laws.

Conclusion

The fundamental cause of bias-motivated violence in the United States is the persistence of racism, bigotry, and anti-Semitism. Unfortunately, there are no quick, complete solutions to these problems. Ultimately, the impact of all bias crime initiatives will be measured in the response of the criminal justice system to the individual act of hate violence. Enactment of the Hate Crime Prevention Act, along with implementation of other hate crime training, prevention, and anti-bias education initiatives announced at the White House Conference on Hate Crimes is, in the language of 18 U.S.C. 245 itself, "in the public interest and necessary to secure substantial justice."

We applaud the leadership of the sponsors of this measure and urge the Judiciary Committee to approve this important legislation as soon as possible.

Anti-Defamation League Model Hate Crime Legislation

Issued by the Anti-Defamation League (ADL), this document surveys the history of the 1981 Model Hate Crime Statute. More than 40 states have enacted this legislation or similar statutes based on this model. This section includes the text of the Model Hate Crime law.

Recognizing that laws shape attitudes as well as behavior, ADL has played a leading role in promoting the enactment and enforcement of federal and state laws to address violent bigotry and counter extremism. Drafted in 1981, ADL model hate crimes legislation is intended to complement other ADL counteraction measures which focus on media exposure, education, and more effective law enforcement.

The ADL model statute has met with a very encouraging response. Currently, at least 40 states and the District of Columbia have enacted laws based on or similar to the ADL model, and almost every state has some form of legislation which can be invoked to redress bias-motivated crimes. The United States Congress has enacted a federal hate crime penalty-enhancement statute as part of the 1994 omnibus crime bill. This provision, the Hate Crimes Sentencing Enhancement Act, required the United States Sentencing Commission to increase the penalties for crimes in which the victim was selected "because of the actual or perceived race, color, religion, national origin, ethnicity, gender, disability, or sexual orientation of any person."

The intent of penalty-enhancement hate crime laws is not only to reassure targeted groups by imposing serious punishment on hate crime perpetrators, but also to deter these crimes by demonstrating that they will be dealt with in a serious manner. Under these laws, no one is punished merely for bigoted thoughts, ideology, or speech. But when prejudice prompts an individual to act on these beliefs and engage in criminal conduct, a prosecutor may seek a more severe sentence, but must prove, beyond reasonable doubt, that the victim was intentionally selected because of his/her personal characteristics.

The ADL model statute also includes an institutional vandalism section which increases the criminal penalties for vandalism aimed at houses of worship, cemeteries, schools and community centers. This provision is useful in dealing with crimes such as the very disturbing series of arsons which have occurred at Black churches across the South over the past two years. The model legislation also creates a civil action for victims and provides for other forms of relief, i.e., recovery of punitive damages and attorneys' fees, and parental liability for minor children's actions. Finally, the statute includes a section on bias-crime reporting and training.

The U.S. Supreme Court's unanimous decision in *Wisconsin v. Mitchell*, 508 U.S. 476 (1993), upholding the constitutionally of the Wisconsin hate crime penalty-enhancement statute based on the ADL model, removed any doubt that state legislatures may properly increase the penalties for criminal activity in which the victim is intentionally targeted because of his/her race, religion, sexual orientation, gender, or ethnicity.

Institutional Vandalism

A. A person commits the crime of institutional vandalism by knowingly vandalizing, defacing or otherwise damaging:

i. Any church, synagogue or other building, structure or place used for religious worship or other religious purpose;

ii. Any cemetery, mortuary or other facility used for the purpose of burial or memorializing the dead;

iii. Any school, educational facility or community center;

iv. The grounds adjacent to, and owned or rented by, any institution, facility, building, structure or place described in subsections (i), (ii) or (iii) above; or

v. Any personal property contained in any institution, facility, building, structure, or place described in subsections (i), (ii) or (iii) above.

B. Institutional vandalism is punishable as follows:

i. Institutional vandalism is a misdemeanor if the person does any act described in subsection A which causes damage to, or loss or, the property of another.

ii. Institutional vandalism is a felony if the person does any act described in Subsection A which causes damage to, or loss of, the property of another in an amount in excess of five hundred dollars.

iii. Institutional vandalism is a felony if the person does any act described in Subsection A which causes damage to, or loss of, property of another in an amount in excess of one thousand five hundred dollars.

iv. Institutional vandalism is a felony if the person does any act described in Subsection A which causes damage to, or loss of, the property of another in an amount in excess of five thousand dollars.

C. In determining the amount of damage to, or loss of, property, damage includes the cost of repair or replacement of the property that was damaged or lost

Bias-Motivated Crimes

A. A person commits a Bias-Motivated Crime if, by reason of the actual or perceived race, color, religion, national origin, sexual orientation or gender of another individual or group of individuals, he violates Section _____ of the Penal code (insert code provisions for criminal trespass, criminal mischief, harassment, menacing, intimidation, assault, battery and or other appropriate statutorily proscribed criminal conduct).

B. A Bias-Motivated Crime under this code provision is a _____ misdemeanor/felony (the degree of criminal liability should be at least one degree more serious than that imposed for commission of the underlying offense).

Civil Action for Institutional Vandalism and Bias-Motivated Crimes

A. Irrespective of any criminal prosecution or result thereof, any person incurring injury to his person or damage or loss to his property as a result of conduct in violation of Sections 1 or 2 of this Act shall have a civil action to secure an injunction, damages or other appropriate relief in law or in equity against any and all persons who have violated Sections 1 or 2 of this Act.

B. In any such action, whether a violation of Sections 1 or 2 of this Act has occurred shall be determined according to the burden of proof used in other civil actions for similar relief.

C. Upon prevailing in such civil action, the plaintiff may recover:

i. Both special and general damages, including damages for emotional distress;

ii. Punitive damages; and/or

iii. Reasonable attorney fees and costs.

A. Notwithstanding any other provision of the law to the contrary, the parent(s) or legal guardian(s) of any unemancipated minor shall be liable for any judgment rendered against such minor under this Section.

Bias Crime Reporting and Training

A. The state police or other appropriate state law enforcement agency shall establish and maintain a central repository for the collection and analysis of information regarding crimes which are motivated by bigotry or bias. Upon establishing such a repository, the state police shall develop a procedure to monitor, record, classify and analyze information relating to crimes apparently directed against individuals or groups, or their property, by reason of their actual or perceived race, color, religion, national origin, sexual orientation or gender. The state police shall submit its procedure to the appropriate committee of the state legislature for approval.

B. All local law enforcement agencies shall report monthly to the state police concerning such offenses in such form and in such manner as prescribed by rules and regulations adopted by state police. The state police must summarize and analyze the information received and file an annual report with the governor and appropriate committee of the state legislature.

C. Any information, records and statistics collected in accordance with this subsection shall be available for use by any local law enforcement agency, unit of local government, or state agency, to the extent that such information is reasonably necessary or useful to such agency in carrying out the duties imposed upon it by law. Dissemination of such information shall be subject to all confidentiality requirements otherwise imposed by law.

D. The state police shall provide training for police officers in identifying, responding to, and reporting all criminal offenses motivated by race, color, religion, national origin, sexual orientation or gender.

Ten Ways to Fight Hate: A Community Response Guide to Hate Crime and Hate Groups

Compiled by Klanwatch, a project of the Southern Poverty Law Center, this widely published pamphlet documents successful methods used by communities throughout the United States to combat hate groups.

Hate comes in many forms.

It can be stark—from anti-Semitic graffiti and the racist chanting of Klansmen to brutal assaults by Skinheads. It can also be subtle—from the reasoned racism of modern neo-Nazi leaders to the pseudo-intellectualism of those who claim that the Holocaust did not occur.

But whatever form it takes, an expression of hatred usually causes an intense reaction in a community.

Although some people argue that hate crimes and hate groups should be ignored, many others look for ways to express their opposition and to send an unequivocal message that racism and bigotry will not be tolerated in their community.

What follows are ten ways to fight hate, drawn from Klanwatch's experience monitoring white supremacist groups and hate crimes and from successful methods used by communities throughout the country.

They are not the only ways to fight hatred, but they are a place to start.

1. Stay Away from White Supremacist Events

When hate groups announce plans to march or rally, people are often unsure about the proper response.

It is tempting, but counterproductive and often dangerous, to confront white supremacists at their public events.

The principal reason is that violence by counterprotesters is becoming commonplace at white supremacist rallies and marches. Some anti-racist demonstrators travel from rally to rally, actually hoping to provoke violent confrontations with the racists. Others may attend the event simply to protest peacefully, only to find themselves enraged by the inflammatory rhetoric and caught up in the violence.

White supremacists are skilled at turning such situations to their advantage, gloating that the violence came from protesters, not the hate group.

In Denver, violence marred the 1992 Martin Luther King holiday when angry protesters at a Klan rally attacked each other, bystanders and police. One anti-Klan demonstrator was seriously injured by another counterprotester, and three police officers were hurt. Twenty-one people were arrested. Order was restored only after police used nightsticks, tear gas and Mace.

At a neo-Nazi rally in Auburn, New York, in September 1993, enraged protesters in a crowd of about 2,000 attacked the racists and pelted police with rocks. The crowd also chased the white supremacists' cars and threw bricks and bottles. Two counterdemonstrators were arrested.

Two Auburn residents, one a Jewish man, rescued a female neo-Nazi after she was struck in the face and kicked. Some of the counterdemonstrators threatened to kill another man who helped the woman.

Finally, it is important to remember that the media often cannot distinguish between curiosity seekers and the hate group's sympathizers when estimating the crowd at white supremacist rallies. Peaceful protesters can easily be mistaken for hate group supporters.

All this can be avoided by simply staying away. Then the event, attended only by white supremacists, will lose much of its appeal to the media.

2. Organize an Alternative Event

To discourage attendance at racist events, communities should organize a multicultural gathering that encourages family participation. Ideally, it should be staged in a different part of the city, at or near the time of the hate group's rally or march.

Examples of such events include the following:

• In Columbus, Ohio, citizens created a Unity Day in response to an October 1993 visit by the Knights of the Ku Klux Klan. Hundreds of people participated in activities that reflected the city's diversity. The program featured rap music, traditional Hebrew songs, a school's Spanish choir, the city's opera and a gay men's chorus. The city used grant money to fund most of the event.

• In Pulaski, Tennessee, the birthplace of the Ku Klux Klan and the site of numerous Klan rallies, residents have countered these events by emphasizing the community's unity and its disgust for the Klan.

On the day of the Klan rally, downtown merchants have closed their businesses and staged a brotherhood march that is now an annual event.

• In Colorado, a ski resort offered discounts on lift tickets and rentals as incentives to keep people away from a 1992 Klan rally.

• Some communities plan ecumenical services where people can express a united front against hate. Such services should incorporate all of the town's religions.

• In Wallingford, Connecticut, townspeople held ecumenical services in December 1993 in response to a series of hate crimes.

• And in Texas, a woman invited 35 churches to a prayer vigil on the same night as a Klan cross-lighting ceremony. "I figured prayer was what these people needed, and a whole bunch of it would be better," she said.

3. Don't Try to Stop White Supremacist Events

People often try to keep white supremacists out of their area by pressuring city officials to deny parade or rally permits.

This tactic is seldom effective. White supremacist groups have won scores of lawsuits on First Amendment grounds against communities that attempted to block their public events.

Ultimately, the event will be held anyway, and the furor surrounding attempts to stop it will only gain more publicity for the hate group.

4. Place Ads in the Local Newspaper

When hate crimes occur, citizens should consider buying an advertisement in the local newspaper.

The ad should emphasize unity and support for the crime victim as well as the target group to which the victim belongs. It should also convey the message that hate crimes will not be tolerated in the community.

Newspaper ads can also counter the publicity that hate groups attract.

These ads should denounce the organization's bigoted views and should run on or before the day of the white supremacist event.

5. Form Community Anti-Racism Groups

Another way to effectively oppose hate groups and hate crime is to form a citizens' anti-racism group. The organization should be composed of people from every race, religion, and culture in the community, including gays and lesbians, who are frequent targets of hate crime and hate groups.

The group should stress cooperation and harmony and discourage confrontational tactics.

Some anti-racism groups, formed in response to a particular racial incident, hate crime or hate group, have found ways to sustain their sense of unity and purpose indefinitely.

One such group, the Friendly Supper Club in Montgomery, Alabama, was founded to ease racial tensions after a violent incident involving city police and black residents.

With the goal of improving the city's strained race relations, black and white residents began meeting over dinner at an inexpensive restaurant to discuss issues affecting the city. There was only one rule—each guest was asked to bring a person of another race to dinner. The Friendly Supper Club has been active since 1983.

6. Respond Quickly to Hate Crimes with a Show of Unity

Concerned citizens should quickly put aside racial, cultural and religious differences and band together to fight the effects of hate crime on a community.

In some areas, non-Jews have joined their Jewish neighbors to scrub swastikas and graffiti off synagogues. Elsewhere, white and black residents have gathered at black churches to remove racial slurs and to rebuild black churches burned by racists.

In mostly white Castro Valley, California, residents organized a unity march in September 1993 after a black teacher's car was vandalized with Klan slogans.

In February 1997, in response to a spate of vicious hate activity on the California State University campus at San Marcos, university employees committed to making donations to an anti-racist organization each time such activity occurs. They made their first donation to the Southern Poverty Law Center.

And in Palm Springs, California, a group of high school students wore ribbons they had made to symbolize unity following a brawl between blacks and Hispanics in October 1993.

"We're trying to show the students who are causing a problem that we're not going to stand by and let that happen," the school's student body president said. "If enough people come together, we can overcome this."

7. Focus on Victim Assistance

Hate crime victims often feel isolated, so it is important to let them know that their community cares about them.

"Network of Neighbors," a volunteer organization formed in 1992 in Pittsburgh, Pennsylvania, offers emotional support to hate crime victims.

Commander Gwen Elliott, head of the Pittsburgh police department's hate crime unit, said the group offers a much-needed service.

"A lot of times, (hate crime victims) don't know how the court system works. They need support and help in dealing with their anger, so they don't go out and do something irrational," Elliott said.

Since hate crimes are not often solved quickly, volunteers should encourage victims to be patient and cooperative with law enforcement officers handling the investigation.

8. Research Hate Crime Laws in Your Community and State

Some states and cities have broad hate crime laws that cover a wide range of incidents. Others have limited statutes that allow only data collection or cover only specific acts of vandalism.

In many states, if a bias crime is prosecuted under a hate crime statute, additional prison time or stiffer fines can be imposed.

Five states have no hate crime laws. In those states, a racial slur written on a black family's house is treated as simple vandalism.

If a community does not have a hate crime law or the existing statute is weak, citizens should urge their elected officials to support strong bias crime legislation.

9. Encourage Multi-Cultural Education in Local Schools

Because more than half of all hate crimes are committed by young people ages 15 to 24, schools should be encouraged to join the fight against hate.

One way is to offer multicultural materials and courses to young people. Educators have learned that once differences are explained, fear and bias produced by ignorance are diminished.

Many schools are already teaching students to understand and respect differences in race, religion, sexual orientation, and culture.

The Southern Poverty Law Center's Teaching Tolerance Project provides educators with workable strategies and ready-to-use materials to help promote tolerance and understanding.

10. Find Unique Ways to Show Opposition

It is important to remember that there is no single right way to fight hate, nor is there any one list, including the one here, of surefire approaches that will work in every community.

The suggested responses in this report should be adapted to local circumstances, and community leaders should always be open to fresh approaches to fighting hate.

With a little imagination, many people have found unique, and often humorous, ways to voice their opposition to bigotry and racism in their communities.

Some recent examples include the following:

• In Connecticut, a community distributed anti-Klan bumper stickers reading, "Our Town is United Against the Klan."

• In Lafayette, Louisiana, the editors of the *Times of Acadiana* said they "felt terrible" about running an advertisement placed by a local chapter of the Ku Klux Klan. So they decided to split the proceeds from the $900 Klan ad between two of the hate group's archenemies—the NAACP and the Southern Poverty Law Center's Klanwatch Project.

Bayou Knights Grand Dragon Roger Harris apparently found the approach a little hard to take. "I have to swallow hard. I really do," Harris said.

• In Springfield, Illinois, a couple gave the Louisiana idea a local twist by turning a January 1994 Klan rally into a fundraising event for three of the Klan's foes—the NAACP, the Anti-Defamation League and the Southern Poverty Law Center.

Based on the adage, "When life gives you a lemon, make lemonade," the event, lightheartedly dubbed Project Lemonade, was modeled after the common walkathon.

The project's donors pledged money for each minute the Klan rally lasted. The longer the rally, the more money was raised for the three anti-racism groups. The project's creators, Bill and Lindy Seltzer, said that the response was excellent and that pledges were collected from throughout the state.

Hate crimes and hate group activity touch everyone in a community. For that reason, people of good will must take a stand to ensure that hatred cannot flourish.

As German Pastor Martin Niemoller said:

In Germany they first came for the Communists and I didn't speak up because I wasn't a Communist. Then they came for the Jews, and I didn't speak up because I wasn't a Jew. Then they came for the trade unionists, and I didn't speak up because I wasn't a trade unionist. Then they came for the Catholics, and I didn't speak up because I was a Protestant.

Then they came for me—and by that time no one was left to speak up.

Directory of Organizations

This chapter includes annotated lists of human and civil rights organizations that monitor both hate crime incidents and extremist groups. The descriptions are mostly derived from the publications and/or Internet sites of the organizations.

American Jewish Committee (AJC)
165 East 56th Street
New York, NY 10022
(212) 751–4000
Internet: http://www.ajc.org/

Founded in 1906, the American Jewish Committee is a membership organization with chapters nationwide. Their programs are guided by the values of Jewish teachings and the principles of American democracy. Committed to working in partnership with the diverse racial, ethnic, and religious groups in the United States, the American Jewish Committee promotes intergroup relations and combats anti-Semitism, racism, and bigotry. On Capitol Hill and in state-houses across the country, the AJC supports legislation mandating severe penalties for hate crimes and the collection of reliable statistics about these incidents. The committee publicized the violent activities of the militia movement before the 1995 Oklahoma City bombing. The AJC publishes *American Jewish Year Book,* an authoritative reference work that covers many aspects of Jewish life including anti-Jewish activities and extremist groups around the world; and *Anti-Semitism World Report,* an annual country-by-country compendium of trends on global anti-Semitism.

Anti-Defamation League (ADL)
823 United Nations Plaza
New York, NY 10017
(212) 490–2525
Internet: http://www.adl.org/

Founded in 1913, the Anti-Defamation League is the preeminent U.S. organization combating anti-Semitism, all forms of bigotry, and discrimination and promoting harmonious relations among diverse religious, ethnic, and racial groups. The ADL's mission is to "stop the defamation of the Jewish people and to secure justice and fair treatment to all citizens alike." National headquarters are in New York City, and there are 32 regional offices throughout the United States. The ADL also has representatives in foreign capitals, including Jerusalem, Vienna, and Rome. The league has been in the forefront of national and state efforts to deter and combat hate-motivated crimes. In 1981, it developed model hate crime statutes that have subsequently been adopted by more than two-thirds of state governments and numerous municipalities throughout the United States. The league's Juvenile Division Project works with the justice system to develop sentencing options for youths who commit bias crimes. The ADL also provides training on hate crimes–related issues to the Federal Bureau of Investigation as well as to law enforcement agencies. \The organization publishes an extensive number of materials on human relations, diversity, and intergroup relations (see Chapters 6 and 7). The following ADL publications specifically address hate crimes: *Audit of Anti-Semitic Incidents*—an annual report documenting anti-Jewish attacks on individuals and property and a survey of the activities of anti-Jewish hate groups; and *Law Enforcement Bulletin*—**a** publication sent to almost 5,000 law enforcement professionals about national and state efforts to curb bias-motivated crimes.

Center for Democratic Renewal (CDR)
P.O. Box 50469
Atlanta, GA 30302
(404) 221–0025

Fax: (404) 221–0045
Internet: http://www.publiceye.org/pra/cdr/aboutcdr.html

Founded in 1979 as the National Anti-Klan Network, the multiracial Center for Democratic Renewal advocates a "democratic, diverse and just society, free of racism and bigotry." The organization formally changed its name in 1985 to reflect its broadened agenda: to serve as a clearinghouse for constructive responses to hate groups and hate-motivated violence. Providing a wide range of programs including research, public education, leadership training, and community organizing, the CDR has also allied itself with other human rights and antiviolence groups to achieve mutual goals. During the 1980s, the CDR worked with farm organizations, churches, and Jewish groups to combat anti-Semitic propaganda aimed at American farmers. The CDR also claims to be the first nongay organization to launch a nationwide campaign against antigay violence. Publications: *When Hate Groups Come to Town*—offers guidelines for community response to local extremist activities; *CDR Activist Updates*—summarizes hate group activity around the country; *Monitor*—the newsletter of the CDR.

Coalition for Human Dignity (CHD)
P.O. Box 40344
Portland, OR 97240
(503) 281–5823
Fax: (503) 281–8673
Internet: http://www.chd-seattle.org/chd/

Established in 1988 in the wake of the murder of Ethiopian student Mulugeta Seraw by neo-Nazi skinheads in Portland, Oregon, the Coalition for Human Dignity initiated research, education, and training programs to combat skinhead violence in Portland and surrounding communities. The organization's goal is to mobilize diverse constituencies and groups to prevent hate-motivated violence and discrimination. The coalition publishes *Northwest Imperative: Documenting a Decade of Hate*—a survey of the activities of almost three dozen hate groups in Oregon, Washington, Idaho, and Montana, published in association with the Northwest Coalition Against Malicious Harassment (see separate entry); and *Dignity Report*—a quarterly journal of investigation and analysis of extremist attacks on civil and human rights.

Klanwatch
400 Washington Avenue
Montgomery, AL 36104
(334) 264–0286
Fax: (334) 264–0629
Internet: http://www.splcenter.org/klanwatch.html

Created by the Southern Poverty Law Center (see separate entry) in 1981 in response to a resurgence of Ku Klux Klan activity, Klanwatch tracks the activities of more than 200 racist and neo-Nazi groups. The organization provides information to law enforcement agencies, the media, and the general public. Staff members conduct training sessions for police and community groups. Publications: *Klanwatch Intelligence Report*—a bimonthly newsletter providing information on racist and KKK activities; *Ku Klux Klan: A History of Racism and Violence; Klanwatch Law Report*—a quarterly publication containing information on litigation and related legal matters.

National Asian Pacific American
Legal Consortium (NAPALC)
1140 Connecticut Avenue N.W.
Washington, DC 20077
(202) 296–2300
Fax: 202–296–2318

The National Asian Pacific American Legal Consortium is a non-profit, nonpartisan organization whose mission is to advance and protect the legal and civil rights of the nation's Asian Pacific Americans through litigation, advocacy, public education, and public policy development. Its priorities include anti-Asian violence prevention and education. The consortium is affiliated with three civil rights legal organizations: Asian American Legal Defense and Education Fund (New York), the Asian Law Caucus (San Francisco), and the Asian Pacific American Legal Center of Southern California (Los Angeles). In their work to address and prevent anti-Asian violence, NAPALC and its affiliates monitor and document hate-motivated violence and educate their community and law enforcement officials about the problem of violent bigotry. The consortium also advocates the passage of strict hate crime laws and defends the constitutionality of hate crime statutes before state and federal courts. The consortium publishes the *NAPALC Audit of Violence Against Asian Pacific Americans*—the only nationwide, nongovernmental compilation and analysis of anti-Asian violence in the United States.

National Gay and Lesbian Task Force (NGLTF)
2320 17th Street NW
Washington, DC 20009–2702
(202) 332–6483
Fax: (202) 332–0207
Internet: http://www.ngtf.org/

The National Gay and Lesbian Task Force is the leading civil rights organization for lesbian, gay, bisexual, and transgender rights. Founded in 1973, the organization combats antigay violence and job discrimination and lobbies for gay rights legislation. In 1984, the NGLTF conducted the first national study focusing exclusively on antigay violence. Two years earlier, the task force created an antiviolence project to promote an official response to violence and harassment perpetrated against individuals because of their sexual orientation. Publications: *Anti-Violence Fact Sheet; Hate Crimes Map; Anti-Violence Organizations List.*

New York City Gay and Lesbian Anti-Violence Project
647 Hudson Street
New York, NY 10014
(212) 807–6761
Fax: (212) 807–1044
Internet: http://www.avp.org/
Hotline: (212) 807–0197 (24 hours)

Although this organization focuses on antigay violence in New York City, the Anti-Violence Project serves as a national clearinghouse for statistics and information on hate crimes motivated by sexual orientation. A member of the National Coalition of Anti-Violence Programs (NCAVP), which was founded in 1995, this group distributes the reports of the national organization through its web site (see address below). The twelfth annual report (1996) on antigay violence was based on documentation provided by local antiviolence programs across the United States. The New York City Gay and Lesbian Anti-Violence Project publishes an occasional newsletter. The NCAVP web site is available at http://www.avp.org/ncavp/1996/index.html.

Northwest Coalition Against Malicious Harassment (NWC)
P.O. Box 16776
Seattle, WA 98116
(206) 233–9136
Fax: (206) 233–0611
Internet: http://www.nwb.net/nwc/

Organized following a Human Rights Celebration rally in July 1986 at a city park in Coeur d'Alene, Idaho, to protest a neo-Nazi conference in nearby Hayden Lake, the Northwest Coalition Against Malicious Harassment includes more than 250 religious, civil rights, labor, and civic groups from Colorado, Idaho, Montana, Oregon, Washington, and Wyoming. The NWC works to foster communities free from malicious harassment, violence, and bigotry based on race, religion, gender, sexual orientation, national origin, and ethnicity. The organization monitors acts of malicious harassment and promotes the passage of legislation to curb hate-motivated violence. The coalition publishes *Northwest Beacon,* a quarterly newsletter distributed to more than 5,000 individuals and groups.

Political Research Associates (PRA)
120 Beacon Street #202
Somerville, MA 02143
(617) 661–9313
Fax: (617) 661–0059
Internet: http://www.publiceye.org/pra/

Political Research Associates was founded in 1981 in Chicago, Illinois, as Midwest Research; in 1987 the organization relocated to the Boston area under its current name. PRA is an independent nonprofit research center that examines the U.S. political right. The organization collects and analyzes information on antidemocratic, authoritarian, and racist right-wing movements and publishes educational resources that explain their ideologies, tactics, agendas, financing, and links to each other. PRA has a library and an extensive publications list, including information packets, topical reports, monographs, and books. Chip Berlet, the senior analyst, has written, edited, and coauthored many PRA publications. *Public Eye* is the organization's newsletter.

Prejudice Institute/Center for the
Applied Study of Ethnoviolence
2743 Maryland Avenue
Baltimore, MD 21218
(410) 830–2435
Fax: (410) 830–2455

Founded in 1984, this nonmembership organization studies the problems of prejudice, discrimination, conflict, and violence. The organization also conducts research on the cause and prevalence of prejudice and violence and their effects on victims and society. Publications: *Campus Ethnoviolence and the Policy Options; Community Response to Bias Crimes and Incidents; The Ecology of Anti-Gay Violence; The Lawyer's Role in Combating Bias-Motivated Violence; Reporting Ethnoviolence;* and *Traumatic Effects of Ethnoviolence.*

Simon Wiesenthal Center
9760 West Pico Boulevard
Los Angeles, CA 90035
(310) 553–9036
Fax: (310) 553–8007
Internet: http://www.wiesenthal.com/

The Simon Wiesenthal Center is an international institute for Holocaust remembrance and the defense of human rights for the Jewish people and other groups. Headquartered in Los Angeles, California, the center's mandate combines social action, public outreach, scholarship, education, and media projects. Center organizers believe that one of the lessons of the Holocaust is the vital importance of tolerance and understanding. The Wiesenthal Center monitors the activities of hate groups and has recently instituted a CyberWatch Action program to mobilize individuals to report hate incidents they have experienced. Their Internet site includes a form to report acts of hatred, including anti-Semitism, racism, or other forms of bigotry. A quarterly publication titled *Response* is distributed to 334,000 members.

Southern Poverty Law Center (SPLC)
P.O. Box 2087
Montgomery, AL 36102
(334) 264–0286
Fax: (334) 264–0629
Internet: http://www.splcenter.org/

Founded in 1971 by Morris Dees and Joe Levin, two southern lawyers, the Southern Poverty Law Center monitors hate activity across the United States, promotes tolerance education, and litigates against violent racist groups. Located in Montgomery, Alabama, the Center's Civil Rights Memorial commemorates 40 individuals who died during the civil rights era. Since 1979, the SPLC has helped victims of racist violence sue for monetary damages by bringing lawsuits against white supremacist organizations. As the result of a 1990 civil suit in response to the killing of Mulugeta Seraw, an Ethiopian student in Oregon, SPLC attorneys won $12.5 million in damages from Tom Metzger and his organization, White Aryan Resistance. Publications include *SPLC Report*, a newsletter (published five times a year) that details organizational activities; and *Teaching Tolerance*, a semiannual publication aimed at educators to promote positive intergroup relations.

Stephen Roth Institute for the Study
of Contemporary Anti-Semitism and Racism
Wiener Library
Tel Aviv University
P.O. Box 39040
Ramat Aviv
Tel Aviv, 69978
Israel
Fax: 972–3–6408383
Internet: http://www.tau.ac.il:81/Anti-Semitism/index.html

This center began operating as the Project for the Study of Anti-Semitism in the fall of 1991 at Tel Aviv University in Israel. Housed in the Wiener Library—one of the world's largest collections of anti-Jewish, Nazi, and extremist literature—the project monitors manifestations of anti-Semitism around the world and operates a computerized database of contemporary anti-Jewish and other hate groups. The database provides needed statistics for an annual report on the current status of anti-Semitism and hate groups, the most recent edition being *Anti-Semitism Worldwide 1997/98*. The project also published *Anti-Semitism in the United States: A National or a Locally Based Phenomenon?* (1996), and *The Jews Cannot Defeat Me: The Anti-Jewish Campaign of Louis Farrakhan and the Nation of Islam* (November 1995).

Print Resources 6

The literature on hate crimes and hate groups is extensive and constantly increasing: it includes books, monographs, journal and magazine articles, and government and nongovernment documents. The following list is necessarily selective and will provide the student and researcher with citations and many annotations to significant publications on the topic.

Books

Allport, Gordon. *The Nature of Prejudice.* Menlo Park, Calif.: Addison-Wesley, 1979 (originally published in 1954).

A pioneering work by a Harvard psychologist on the social and psychological nature of bigotry.

Barkun, Michael. *Religion and the Racist Right: The Origins of the Christian Identity Movement.* Chapel Hill: University of North Carolina, 1994.

A survey and analysis of the Christian Identity movement, a racist and anti-Jewish ideology whose adherents claim as a religion.

Bellant, Russ. *Old Nazis, the New Right and the Republican Party.* Boston: South End, 1991.

A disturbing investigation of the heretofore unknown ties of former Nazis who immigrated to this country after World War II and established ties to mainstream political groups.

Blee, Kathleen. *Women of the Klan: Racism and Gender in the 1920s.* Berkeley: University of California Press, 1991.

An innovative work examining the involvement of women in America's most notorious racist organization. The author, a professor of women's studies and sociology at the University of Pittsburgh, found that some of these women were involved with women's suffrage and other progressive movements. She interviewed many former members living in the Midwest.

Cleary, Edward J. *Beyond the Burning Cross: The First Amendment and the Landmark R. A. V. Case.* New York: Random House, 1994.

An extensive discussion of the legal ramifications of the Supreme Court case involving a hate crime in St. Paul, Minnesota, in 1992.

Coates, James. *Armed and Dangerous: The Rise of the Survivalist Right.* New York: Hill and Wang, 1995.

An investigative reporter for the *Chicago Tribune,* Coates has written an informative survey of the main organizations and individuals on the violent wing of America's extreme political right. A preface to this edition updates events since its initial publication in 1987. Especially noteworthy is the bibliographic notes section providing access to a wide variety of relevant newspaper and magazine articles and books published in the 1980s.

Comstock, Gary David. *Violence Against Lesbians and Gay Men.* New York: Columbia University Press, 1991.

This study provides statistical data on the nationwide extent of antigay violence and offers a theoretical framework to examine its origins. The book includes a chapter on police violence and empirical data on perpetrators. Also contains extensive footnotes and a bibliography.

Dees, Morris, and Steve Fiffer. *Hate on Trial: The Case Against*

America's Most Dangerous Neo-Nazi. New York: Villard Books, 1993.

The story of the lawsuit brought by a founder of the Southern Poverty Law Center against Tom Metzger, a neo-Nazi, who instigated the murder of an Ethiopian student in Portland, Oregon. Metzger and his skinhead group were required to pay a multi-million dollar settlement to the family of the murdered African immigrant.

Dobratz, Betty A., and Stephanie L. Shanks-Meile. *White Power, White Pride: The White Separatist Movement in the United States.* New York: Twayne, 1997.

This work examines the "white separatist movement" through extensive interviews with more than 100 active participants. The authors attended rallies and other gatherings to chronicle the history and strategies of the movement.

Dyer, Joel. *Harvest of Rage: Why the Oklahoma City Bombing Is Only the Beginning.* Boulder, Colo.: Westview, 1997.

Dyer, a Colorado journalist, surveys the rise of violent antigovernment and extremist hate groups to better understand the attitudes that resulted in the horrific bombing of the federal building in Oklahoma City in 1995, killing 168 people.

Ezekiel, Raphael S. *The Racist Mind: Portraits of American Neo-Nazis and Klansmen.* New York: Vintage, 1995.

A senior research scientist at the Harvard School of Public Health, Ezekiel spent four years conducting extensive interviews with members of a neo-Nazi group and leaders of racist organizations in order to understand the origin of their views.

Ferrell, Claudine L. *Nightmare and Dream: Anti-Lynching in Congress, 1917–1922.* New York: Garland, 1986.

Originally a doctoral dissertation, this work surveys legislative initiatives in Congress to end the wave of Southern lynchings during the early part of the twentieth century.

Foster, Arnold. *Square One.* New York: Donald I. Fine, 1988.

A memoir by the former general counsel of the Anti-Defamation League describes his life-long battle against anti-Semitism and his concern for the welfare and rights of the Jewish people.

Hamm, Mark S. *American Skinheads: The Criminology and Control of Hate Crime.* Westport, Conn.: Praeger, 1993.

This volume examines the social and psychological dimensions of the skinhead movement and analyzes its development through interviews with some members. According to the author, "not all acts of terrorism can be considered hate crimes, and hate crimes are not necessarily terrorism unless such prejudiced violence has a political or social underpinning."

———. *Hate Crime: International Perspectives on Causes and Control.* Highland Heights, Ky.: Academy of Criminal Justice Sciences, Northern Kentucky University; and Cincinnati, Ohio: Anderson Publishing Co., 1994.

Hentoff, Nat. *Free Speech for Me—But Not for Thee: How the American Left and Right Relentlessly Censor Each Other.* New York: HarperCollins, 1992.

Hentoff, a prolific writer on civil liberties, presents an absolutist interpretation of the First Amendment to the U.S. Constitution.

Herek, Gregory M., and Kevin T. Berrill. *Hate Crimes: Confronting Violence Against Lesbians and Gay Men.* Newbury Park, Calif.: Sage Publications, 1992.

The first major monograph on antigay violence in the United States, this anthology includes an overview of the topic, essays on perpetrators and victims, and also suggestions for public policy responses. Data and analysis from the first national study conducted by the National Gay and Lesbian Task Force in 1984 are presented.

Israel, Constance Denney. *Hate Crimes Against Gays/Lesbians in the Mainstream Press: An Examination of Six Texas Dailies.* Las Colinas, Tex.: Monument Press, 1992.

This book was originally presented as the author's thesis for a M.A. degree at the University of Texas in 1991.

Jacobs, James B., and Kimberly Potter. *Hate Crimes: Criminal Law and Identity Politics.* New York: Oxford University Press, 1998.

James B. Jacobs, a New York law professor and pre-eminent critic of hate crimes legislation, along with his coauthor, argues that these laws are both subjective and unnecessary and infringe on basic First Amendment rights. An important critical contribution to the hate crimes debate.

Jenness, Valerie, and Kendal Broad. *Hate Crimes: New Social Movements and the Politics of Violence.* New York: Aldine de Gruyter, 1997.

This work examines why bias-motivated violence has recently become a serious issue and the reason some minority constituencies have been categorized as victims while others have gone relatively unnoticed. A sociopolitical analysis, the book also discusses the response to violence against gays and women.

Kelly, Robert J., ed. *Bias Crime: American Law Enforcement and Legal Responses.* Chicago: Office of International Criminal Justice, University of Illinois at Chicago, 1993.

This is an anthology covering various methods used by police and other law enforcement officials to prosecute violent hate crimes. Although much of the material covers the mid- and late 1980s, it still provides a useful overview for government attorneys, prosecutors, and other public officials.

Kotlowitz, Alex. *The Other Side of the River: A Story of Two Towns, A Death, and America's Dilemma.* New York: Nan A. Talese/Doubleday, 1998.

When the Coast Guard pulled the body of Eric McGinnis, a black teenager, out of southwestern Michigan's St. Joseph's River in May 1991, the mostly white residents of St. Joseph assumed the drowning was accidental. But African Americans in Benton Harbor, a mostly black town on the other side of the river, believed that whites chased him into the water for dating a white girl and that the crime was covered up by the white-dominated St. Joseph police force. Written by the author of the award-winning book *There Are No Children Here,* this work deals brilliantly with how differing perceptions of events are filtered through one's racial background.

Lamy, Philip. *Millennium Rage.* New York: Plenum Press, 1996.

Ultra–right-wing groups and militias are flourishing as the year 2000 approaches. The author, a professor at Castleton State College in Vermont, examines the growth of this movement.

Levin, Jack, and Jack McDevitt. *Hate Crimes.* New York: Plenum Press, 1993.

This work surveys the growth of hate-motivated violence in the United States during the 1980s and early 1990s. The authors advocate concerted community response to deter these crimes.

MacLean, Nancy. *Behind the Mask of Chivalry: The Making of the Second Ku Klux Klan.* New York: Oxford University Press, 1994.

This work discusses the rebirth of the KKK and its attitude toward white women, blacks, Catholics, Jews, and immigrants and how it implements its policy of terror through lynching and other violent crimes.

Martinez, Thomas, with John Guinther. *Brotherhood of Murder.* New York: McGraw-Hill, 1988.

A first-person account by a former member of the neo-Nazi group The Order. After Martinez revealed the organization's activities to federal law enforcement agencies, his ex-comrades threatened his life.

Newton, Michael and Judy, eds. *Ku Klux Klan: An Encyclopedia.* New York: Garland, 1991.

Probably the only event worth commemorating on the 125th anniversary of the "world's oldest, most persistent terrorist organization" is the publication of this outstanding reference source. Meticulous and diligent researchers, the Newtons have compiled an essential guide for students and researchers.

———. *Racial and Religious Violence in America: A Chronology.* New York: Garland, 1991.

An outstanding reference source providing a chronology of many violent bias-motivated incidents throughout American history.

Ridgeway, James. *Blood in the Face: The Ku Klux Klan, Aryan Nations, Nazi Skinheads, and the Rise of a New White Culture.* New York: Thunder's Mouth Press, 1995.

In this updated second edition, a *Village Voice* journalist surveys the rise of violent racist groups throughout the country. The book is well illustrated with photographs and artwork; especially noteworthy is a chart showing the interrelationships among the various groups and individuals. The author has filmed a documentary in conjunction with this work.

Robins, Robert S., and Jerrold M. Post. *Political Paranoia: The Psychopolitics of Hatred.* New Haven: Yale University Press, 1997.

Written by a political scientist and psychiatrist, this work surveys the phenomenon of the paranoid personality and how it generates various political and social movements. Hitler, Stalin, Christian Identity, and the Nation of Islam are some of the topics discussed in this wide-ranging work.

Sargent, Lyman Tower, ed. *Extremism in America: A Reader.* New York: New York University Press, 1995.

This unique anthology contains the actual texts of the hard-to-locate publications, articles, and tracts issued from both ends of the political spectrum—the far left and far right. The work is conveniently organized by topic, including race, gender, economics, and education.

Sims, Patsy. *The Klan.* Lexington: University Press of Kentucky, 1996.

Surveys the history and recent activities of this notorious organization based on interviews with current members.

Smith, Brent L. *Terrorism in America: Pipe Bombs and Pipe Dreams.* New York: State University of New York Press, 1994.

The author, a professor of criminal justice and sociology at the University of Alabama, provides empirical data and analysis of left-wing and right-wing terrorist groups in the United States.

Stanton, Bill. *Klanwatch: Bringing the Ku Klux Klan to Justice.* New York: Grove Weidenfeld, 1991.

The former director of the Southern Poverty Law Center's Klanwatch Project chronicles the history of his organization's "multi-pronged anti-Klan program," which included filing lawsuits, publishing educational materials, and monitoring the activities of the KKK. Engagingly written, the book contains several photographs.

Tunnell, Kenneth D. *Political Crime in Contemporary America: A Critical Approach.* New York: Garland Publishing, 1993.

Contains a chapter by Wayman C. Mullins, editor of the *Journal of Police and Criminal Psychology,* entitled "Hate Crime and the Far Right."

Vollers, Maryanne. *Ghosts of Mississippi: The Murder of Medgar Evers, the Trials of Byron De La Beckwith, and the Haunting of the New South.* Boston: Little Brown and Company, 1995.

Provides background to the murder conviction of a white supremacist in the 1963 murder of the NAACP leader Medgar Evers. After two mistrials, Beckwith was convicted in 1992.

Wade, Wyn Craig. *The Fiery Cross: The Ku Klux Klan in America.* New York: Simon and Schuster, 1987.

Walker, Samuel. *Hate Speech: The History of an American Controversy.* Lincoln: University of Nebraska Press, 1994.

The author, a professor of criminal justice at the University of Nebraska at Omaha, surveys the history of hate speech from the 1920s to the present and the varying views about suppressing it from organizations ranging from the American Civil Liberties Union to the American Jewish Committee and the NAACP.

Wang, Lu-In. *Hate Crimes Law.* Deerfield, Ill.: Clark Boardman Callaghan, 1994– (with annual updates).

A comprehensive reference source on the federal and state statutes enacted to address bias-motivated hate crimes. An outstanding and essential work for law students, law enforcement officials, scholars, and researchers.

Whitfield, Stephen J. *A Death in the Delta: The Story of Emmett Till.* New York: Free Press, 1988.

A meritorious work that deserves wider recognition. The book recounts the story of a black teenager who was murdered in Money, Mississippi, in 1955 for allegedly whistling at a white female. Many historians view this incident as the beginning of the modern civil rights movement.

Winters, Paul A., ed. *Hate Crimes.* San Diego: Greenhaven Press, 1996.

A useful anthology composed of a wide variety of material reprinted from periodicals, newspapers, books, and private organizations. Also contains an excellent introductory essay.

Articles

Alvarez, Lizette. **"After Blaze, Mourning Loved Ones."** *New York Times*, December 13, 1995: B8.

The families of the victims of the fatal fire at Freddy's Fashion Mart in Harlem mourn their relatives.

Anderson, George M. **"People Are Getting Hurt: The Rise in Gay-Bashing."** *Commonweal*, February 23, 1993: 16–17.

The author is alarmed at the increase in hate crimes against gays, which he believes is partly inspired by religious teaching against homosexuality.

Annual Survey of American Law, 1992/93. Issue Number 4, New York University School of Law.

Contains the papers given at a special symposium held at the New York University School of Law on November 12, 1993. This conference brought together scholars and lawyers from across the country to discuss the "propriety, practicality and constitutionality of burgeoning hate crime statutes." Especially notable are the essays by NYU Professor Lawrence Crocker (pp. 485–507) and Columbia University Professor Kent Greenawalt (pp. 617–628).

"Anti-Arab Violence Up in U.S., Group Says." *New York Times*, February 24, 1992: A15.

The article summarizes a report issued by the American Arab Anti-Discrimination Committee.

Applebome, Peter. **"Rise Is Found in Hate Crimes Committed by Blacks."** *New York Times*, December 13, 1993: A12.

According to a Klanwatch report, 46 percent of all racially motivated killings were committed by blacks against victims who were white, Asian, or Hispanic. Morris Dees, the president of the Southern Poverty Law Center, said that as recently as the 1980s, it was extremely rare to find black perpetrators of hate crimes. He distinguished criminal activity such as robbery from violent criminal acts motivated by antagonism to a person because of race or ethnicity.

"Bad Motives." Editorial, *New Yorker,* June 21, 1993: 4–5.

This editorial asserts that hate crime laws are counterproductive. Minorities are often the target of hate crime prosecution, and the search for a motive could violate the constitutional rights of a suspect.

Bader, Hans F. **"Penalty Enhancement for Bias-Based Crimes."** *Harvard Journal of Law and Public Policy,* Winter 1994: 253–262.

Although the U.S. Supreme Court found the penalty enhancement hate crime statute in Wisconsin constitutional, it left unresolved the treatment of crimes that mix speech and conduct. State legislatures may use this ambiguity to restrict the expression of dissident opinions.

Barnes, Arnold, and Paul H. Ephross. **"The Impact of Hate Violence on Victims: Emotional and Behavioral Responses to Attacks."** *Social Work,* May 1994: 247–251.

This journal article examines the nature of hate violence and its effect on 59 victims (aged 16–67 years old) who were victimized by hate crimes. The data were derived from group meetings, individual interviews, and questionnaires. Most victims had experienced several attacks and reacted with anger, fear, and sadness. About one-third of the subjects moved from their former neighborhoods or bought a weapon for self-defense. The author suggests that social workers should help victims manage the stress resulting from these crimes.

Behar, Richard. **"Warlocks, Witches and Swastikas: A Forgiving Rabbi Tries to Enlighten the Four Teenagers Who Defaced His Home and Temple."** *Time,* October 29, 1990: 27–28.

Discusses how Rabbi Eugene Markovitz of Clifton, New Jersey, dealt with teenagers who committed a hate crime against him and his community.

Belgum, Deborah. **"Impact of Hate Crimes Recounted at Summit."** *Los Angeles Times,* November 13, 1997: B3.

This article discusses the tensions between African Americans and Hispanic Americans in Los Angeles County, California.

Bennet, James. **"Clinton Convenes Conference on Hate Crimes."** *New York Times*, November 11, 1997: A20.

A news article on the first White House Conference on Hate Crimes.

———. **"Jewish Couple Is Beaten in Brooklyn Bias Incident."** *New York Times*, February 8, 1992: 24.

Israel and Yaffa Aminov, Jewish immigrants from the former Soviet Union, are victims of hate violence in Brooklyn, New York.

"Bias-Incited Beating Death of a Vietnamese Stuns a Florida Town." *New York Times*, August 23, 1992: 35.

Luyen Phan Nguyen, a premed student at the University of Miami, is beaten to death by a group of white teenagers motivated by anti-Asian sentiment in Coral Springs, Florida.

Birnbaum, Jesse. **"When Hate Makes a Fist."** *Time*, April 26, 1993: 30–31.

A discussion of hate crime laws and the Supreme Court decisions.

Bowles, Julie Makinen. **"Reports of Anti-Gay Violence in D.C. Area."** *Washington Post*, March 4, 1998: B3.

According to the District of Columbia organization Gay Men and Lesbians Opposing Violence, there has been a 25 percent increase in violence committed against gay people from 1996 to 1997. This report claims that 40 percent of these incidents are never reported to the police.

Boyd, Elizabeth A. **"Motivated by Hatred or Prejudice: Categorization of Hate-Motivated Crimes in Two Police Divisions."** *Law and Society Review*, November 1996: 819–850.

This article examines how police detectives in a large urban police department categorize hate crimes and how their methods affect the reporting of the crimes and the compilation of summary statistics.

Brooke, James. **"Killing Wasn't Much, Skinhead Says: Slaying of West African Leaves Denver Stunned and Frightened."** *New York Times*, November 22, 1997: A7.

The slaying of Oumar Dia, a Mauritanian by a white skinhead alarms the mile-high city residents.

Brozan, Nadine. **"Anti-Gay Violence Rises in 6 Cities, Study Finds."** *New York Times*, March 7, 1991:B8.

A summary of a report issued by the National Gay and Lesbian Task Force Policy Institute.

Cacas, Samuel R. **"Hate Crime Sentences Can Now Be Enhanced Under a New Federal Law."** *Human Rights* (ISSN 0046-8185), Winter 1995: 32–33.

This article reviews provisions of the September 1994 federal crime bill, which allows sentences to be increased if they are motivated by hatred of the victim's race, religion, sexual orientation, national origin, ethnicity, gender, or disability.

"California Anti-Bias Department Firebombed in New Hate Attack." *New York Times*, October 15, 1993: A24.

A neo-Nazi and white supremacist group, the Aryan Liberation Front claimed responsibility for bombing the California Employment and Housing Department. Members of this racist group have also been linked to firebombings aimed at Jewish, black, and Japanese-American targets.

"A Case of an Ethnic Attack Is Called a Hoax." *New York Times*, November 4, 1995: 9.

An Iranian woman in Fargo, North Dakota is suspected of starting a fire herself, which she initially claimed was a hate crime.

"Cause of Deaths Reported." *New York Times*, December 12, 1995: A11.

Law enforcement officials investigate the death of two lesbians in Medford, Oregon in a suspected hate crime.

Chua-Eoan, Howard. **"Enlisted Killers: A Double Murder Raises the Specter of Race Hatred in the Military."** *Time*, December 18, 1995: 44.

Jackie Burden and Michael James, two African Americans, were killed in Fayette, North Carolina, in a random hate crime committed by Army officers with ties to white supremacist groups.

Clarke, Floyd I. **"Hate Violence in the United States."** *FBI Law Enforcement Bulletin*, January 1991: 14–18.

Written shortly after the FBI was mandated to compile statistics on hate crimes, this article surveys bias-motivated crimes throughout the country.

"Close the Hate Crime Loophole." Editorial, *New York Times,* May 3, 1993: A14.

An editorial view of the U.S. Supreme Court decision on the Minnesota hate crime statute.

Cooke, Leonard. **"Fighting Hate Crimes: The Eugene Model."** *The Police Chief,* October 1994: 44–47.

The Police Services Division of the Department of Public Safety in Eugene, Oregon, claims success in protecting the civil rights of minorities and deterring hate crimes. The division has fostered an excellent working relationship with minority groups and also other law enforcement agencies.

Corelli, Rae. **"A Tolerant Nation's Hidden Shame: A Federal Study Suggests That Thousands May Be Victims of Hate Crime."** *Maclean's,* August 14, 1995: 40–43.

A survey of hate crimes directed against Jews, Blacks, native people, gay men, and lesbians in Canada.

Craig, Kellina M. **"So What's a Hate Crime Anyway? Young Adults' Perceptions of Hate Crimes, Victims, and Perpetrators."** *Law and Human Behavior,* April 1996: 113–129.

In this study, male and female students respond to various questions about hate crimes. The results indicate that the students hold various definitions of hate crimes and that their perceptions of bigoted activity vary according to demographic background. The study finds the need for more public awareness and education regarding hate crimes.

"Crime and Punishment." Editorial, *The New Republic,* October 12, 1992: 7.

The journal believes that a hate crimes bill submitted by U.S. Representative Charles A. Schumer (D-NY) is well meaning but may be unconstitutional.

Czajkoski, Eugene H. **"Criminalizing Hate: An Empirical Assessment."** *Federal Probation* (ISSN 0014-9128), September 1992: 36–40.

This study of 259 incidents officially reported during the first year of the Florida Hate Crimes Reporting Act indicated that the typical hate crime is racially motivated, committed against a person instead of property, and usually involves a male against another adult male.

Dees, Morris. **"Taking Hate Groups to Court."** *Trial* (ISSN 0041-2538), February 1995: 20–29.

Written by the cofounder of the Southern Poverty Law Center, this article discusses his innovative legal method of filing civil lawsuits against hate crime perpetrators.

————. **"Young, Gullible and Taught to Hate."** *New York Times*, August 25, 1993: A15.

The author explains how white supremacist groups recruit skinheads to carry out violent hate crimes.

"Dinkins to List Bias Crimes Against Homosexuals in City." *New York Times*, March 5, 1991: B4.

Mayor David Dinkins of New York City, a strong supporter of civil rights for all minorities, instituted this program to alert the public about antigay violence.

Dority, Barbara. **"The Criminalization of Hatred."** *The Humanist*, May-June 1994: 38–39.

The author criticizes hate crime laws, which she believes cannot solve the problem but instead may violate civil liberties.

Feingold, Stanley. **"Hate Crime Legislation Muzzles Free Speech."** *National Journal*, July 12, 1993: 15.

The author does not believe that hate crime laws reduce bigotry; he also thinks the number of protected victim categories is expanding too rapidly.

Fernandez, Joseph M. **"Bringing Hate Crime into Focus: The Hate Crime Statistics Act of 1990."** *Harvard Civil-Rights–Civil-Liberties Review*, Winter 1991: 261–293.

A legislative overview and analysis of the first federal law mandating the U.S. government to collect hate crime data.

"The Few, Not the Guilty." *Time*, April 26, 1993: 16.

Three Marines are acquitted on charges of beating a gay man.

"First Amendment—Bias-Motivated Crimes—Court Strikes Down Hate Crimes Penalty Enhancer Statute." Legal Case note, *Harvard Law Review*, February 1993: 957–962.

A legal analysis of the Wisconsin Supreme Court decision on hate crime statutes.

Fried, Joseph P. **"A Murder Verdict Becomes A Rallying Cry."** *New York Times*, November 24, 1991: E6.

The conviction of the murderer of Julio Rivera, a gay man, heartens many gay activists.

————. **"Victim Recalls Howard Beach and the Attack."** *New York Times*, September 26, 1990: B3.

Cedric Sandiford testifies at the trial of three white men accused in the infamous Howard Beach incident of 1986.

Fumento, Michael. **"*USA Today*'s Arson Artistry."** *American Spectator*, December 1996: 28–33.

Investigative journalist Michael Fumento claims that *USA Today* helped publicize a "faux epidemic" of black church burnings. The author also charges that much of the money raised was channeled to liberal groups and not for the rebuilding of these churches.

Gallagher, John. **"Hate Crime."** *Advocate* (ISSN 0001-8996), July 11, 1995: 30–34.

Discusses an attack on gay men in Sioux City, Iowa, which the police declined to initially classify as a hate crime.

Galst, Liz. **"Taking It to the Streets: Nationwide Queer Street Patrols Come Out Against AntiLesbian and AntiGay Violence."** *Advocate* (ISSN 0001-8996), November 5, 1991: 66–67.

Several gay organizations have organized street patrols to supplement police patrols in their community.

Gannon, Julie. **"We Can't Afford Not to Fight: Morris Dees Takes Bigotry to Court."** *Trial* (ISSN 0041-2538), January 1997: 18–24.

An interview with the cofounder and chief trial counsel for the Southern Poverty Law Center.

"Gay Sailor Tells of a 'Living Hell': Slain Homosexual's Shipmate Recalls Daily Harassment on Both Ship and Base." *New York Times*, March 8, 1993: A15.

This article reports on the vicious slaying of Allen R. Schindler, a sailor who was brutally beaten to death by a fellow Navy officer.

Gellman, Susan. **"Sticks and Stones Can Put You in Jail, but Can Words Increase Your Sentence? Constitutional and Policy Dilemmas of Ethnic Intimidation Laws."** *UCLA Law Review* 39 (December 1991): 333–396.

Gellman, a leading legal critic of hate crimes legislation, provides a critical analysis of the constitutional problems with these statutes.

Gerstenfeld, Phyllis B. **"Smile When You Call Me That: The Problems with Punishing Hate-Motivated Behavior."** *Behavioral Sciences and the Law*, Spring 1992: 259–285.

The author, a professor at the University of Nebraska-Lincoln, argues that there are many practical and policy problems with hate crime laws. She believes that policymakers should pursue other means of reducing hate-motivated activities.

Goldberg, Casey. **"Shunning 'He' and 'She,' They Fight for Respect."** *New York Times*, September 8, 1996: 24.

Discusses transgendered and transsexual individuals who are seeking protection from discrimination and hate crimes.

Goldberg, Suzanne B., and Bea Hanson. "**Violence Against Lesbians and Gay Men.**" *Clearinghouse Review*, Special Issue 1994: 417–431.

Gonzalez, David. **"Joining Hands to Rebuild Church Ruins."** *New York Times*, June 19, 1996: B1.

The New York Board of Rabbis established a fund to help rebuild burned African American churches.

Greenberg, Sally J. **"Massachusetts Hate Crime Reporting Act of 1990: Great Expectations yet Unfulfilled?"** *New England Law Review*, Fall 1996: 103–158.

This article compares hate crimes statutes in Massachusetts with other New England states and also discusses the criteria for reporting these incidents.

Greenhouse, Linda. **"Justices Uphold Stiffer Sentences for Hate Crimes: Wisconsin Law Affirmed; Unanimous Decision Clears up Confusion in Debate over Freedom of Expression."** *New York Times,* June 12, 1993: 1.

A news story about the landmark U.S. Supreme Court decision on hate crimes, including excerpts from the decision.

Greer, Colin. **"How to Fight Hate Crimes."** *Parade Magazine,* February 23, 1997, cover story.

The main feature story in this Sunday syndicated newspaper supplement highlights how communities throughout the country have rallied against bigotry and hate-motivated violence.

Haberman, Clyde. **"An Affront to the Dead, and the Living."** *New York Times,* June 13, 1997:B1.

This article discusses the desecration of a Jewish cemetery in Queens, New York.

"Hate Crime." Editorial, *New Republic,* April 3, 1995: 10.

Discusses the television program *The Jenny Jones Show,* which featured a gay person who was later murdered by another guest.

"Hate Crime Problem." Editorial, *Washington Post,* November 17, 1997: A22.

"Hate Crime Problem. (Cont'd)." Editorial, *Washington Post,* December 1, 1997:A24.

"Hate Crimes Declined in 1994, FBI Says." *New York Times,* November 16, 1995: A18.

The article summarizes the major findings in the 1994 *FBI Hate Crime Statistics* annual report.

"Hate Is Not Speech: A Constitutional Defense of Penalty Enhancement for Hate Crimes." *Harvard Law Review,* April 1993: 1314–1331.

A legal and constitutional defense for state hate crime statutes. This article criticizes the U.S. Supreme Court decision in *R. A. V. v. City of St. Paul,* which struck down a local ordinance against bias-motivated crime.

Hentoff, Nat. **"Multiculturalism and Free Speech."** *The Progressive,* November 1992: 15–18.

A prolific writer on civil liberties, Nat Hentoff argues that hate crime laws and speech codes designed to limit hate speech are violations of the First Amendment.

Herdt, Gilbert. **"The Protection of Gay and Lesbian Youth."** *Harvard Educational Review,* Summer 1995: 315–321.

This essay reviews two books—*Hate Crimes* by Jack Levin and Jack McDevitt, and *Violence Against Lesbians and Gay Men* by Gary David Comstock (see above entries)—concentrating on the treatment of violence and homophobia in these works.

Herek, Gregory M. **"Hate Crime Victimization Among Lesbian, Gay and Bisexual Adults."** *Journal of Interpersonal Violence,* April 1997: 195–215.

Interviews with almost 150 victims of antigay violence in Sacramento, California, indicate that they manifest higher levels of depression, anxiety, anger, and post-traumatic stress than other crime victims.

Hernandez, Greg. **"Supremacist Sentenced to Death for Hate Crime."** *Los Angeles Times,* December 13, 1997: A1.

Gunner Lindberg, 22 years old, is reportedly the first person to be sentenced to death in California for committing a murder motivated by racial hatred. He brutally beat to death Thien Minh Ly, a Vietnamese honor student.

Hernandez, Tanya-Kateri. **"Bias Crimes: Unconscious Racism in the Prosecution of Racially Motivated Violence."** *Yale Law Journal,* January 1990: 845–864.

Written before most hate crime legislation was enacted, this article advocates the need for local and federal laws to deter these crimes.

Hicks, Jonathan P. **"Bias Crimes Include the Disabled: Expanded to Cover Anyone with AIDS."** *New York Times,* April 21, 1993: B3.

Discusses a New York City statute that protects individuals infected with the AIDS virus.

"Hidden Hate." Editorial, *National Review,* April 8, 1996: 18.

The editorial claims that the media underreports black hate crimes committed against whites and other groups.

Holloway, Lynette. **"Five Men Beat Hasidic Artist in Brooklyn in Possible Bias Incident."** *New York Times*, December 25, 1992: B2.

Discusses the beating of Shmuel Graybar, a Hasidic Jew, by black assailants in the Ebbets Field Houses in the Crown Heights section of Brooklyn, New York.

"Home-Grown Hatemongers." *New York Times*, February 27, 1991: A26.

The editorial urges President George Bush to forcefully condemn hate crimes committed against Arab Americans during the Gulf War.

Horowitz, Craig. **"The New Anti-Semitism."** *New York Magazine*, January 11, 1993: 20–28.

This article surveys a rash of anti-Jewish incidents in New York City.

Idelson, Holly. **"Hate-Crimes Bill Drawing Reluctant Opposition."** *Congressional Quarterly Weekly Report*, March 6, 1993: 521.

Discusses congressional opposition to hate crimes legislation from some lawmakers who believe that it punishes freedom of speech.

"In Philadelphia, Race Is Issue in Assault Trial." *New York Times*, January 27, 1998: A9.

Some white residents are accused of assaulting a black woman and members of her family in the City of Brotherly Love.

Jacobs, James B. **"Rethinking the War Against Hate Crimes: A New York City Perspective."** *Criminal Justice Ethics*, Summer-Fall 1992: 55–61.

The New York City Police Department established a Bias Crime Unit in 1980 to keep track of hate crimes. This unit has found that most perpetrators of these crimes are teenage gangs or individuals, not organized racist groups.

————. **"Should Hate Be a Crime?"** *The Public Interest*, Fall 1993: 3–15.

The author, a New York University law professor, criticizes hate crime laws on legal, political, and criminological grounds.

————. **"The Social Construction of a Hate Crime Epidemic."** *Journal of Criminal Law and Criminology*, Winter 1996: 366–391.

A prolific writer on the topic, Professor Jacobs criticizes advocacy groups that claim the United States has been experiencing an "epidemic" of hate crimes. He believes their statistical reports are unreliable and lack credibility. Professor Jacobs particularly refutes charges that the situation has grown worse in recent years; he briefly surveys the historical treatment of African Americans, Jews, and others and believes that the nation is, in fact, more intolerant now of hate crimes than at any other time in our history.

Jacobs, James B., and Barry Eisler. **"Hate Crime Statistics Act of 1990."** *Criminal Law Bulletin*, March-April 1993: 99–123.

A legal analysis of the first federal law mandating the collection of hate crime statistics by the U.S. government.

Jacobs, James B., and Kimberly A. Potter. **"Hate Crimes: A Critical Perspective."** In *Crime and Justice: A Review of Research*, Michael Tonry, ed. (Chicago: University of Chicago Press, 1997): 1-50.

Although it is written from the perspective of a critic of hate crimes legislation, this essay provides an excellent overview of the topic and a very useful bibliography.

Janofsky, Michael. **"Review at Fort Bragg Finds Few Supremacists."** *New York Times*, December 13, 1995: B12.

An internal U.S. Army review found no large-scale involvement in white supremacist and neo-Nazi groups at the North Carolina army base.

————. **"Victims of Bias Try to Steer Skinheads Off Road to Hate."** *New York Times*, January 1, 1994: 1.

Marc R. Greenberg, an assistant U.S. attorney in Los Angeles, California, required white skinheads convicted of bombing a synagogue and other hate crimes to attend a counseling program. Some of the instructors were Jewish Holocaust survivors.

Johnston, David. **"Hostility Toward Arabs and Jews Is Found on Rise."** *New York Times*, February 7, 1991: A22.

Jones, Timothy R. **"Klansmen Wise Up."** *Christianity Today*, July 16, 1990: 13.

Members of the Klan convicted of racial violence are ordered to attend reeducation classes.

Jost, Kenneth. **"Hate Crimes: Are Longer Sentences for Hate Crimes Constitutional?"** *CQ Researcher,* January 8, 1993: 1–24.

This issue surveys the history of hate crimes legislation and the legal, political, and social ramifications of the problem. An excellent overview of the topic.

Kelly, Michael. **"Playing with Fire."** *New Yorker,* July 15, 1996: 28–36.

An award-winning journalist and former editor of the *New Republic,* Michael Kelly disputes the widely publicized claims that the church burnings were entirely racist incidents. Early investigations show that some of the perpetrators are mentally unbalanced or common criminals.

Kibelstis, Teresa Eileen. **"Preventing Violence Against Gay Men and Lesbians: Should Enhanced Penalties at Sentencing Extend to Bias Crimes Based on Victims' Sexual Orientation?"** *Notre Dame Journal of Law, Ethics and Public Policy,* volume IX, issue, no. 1, 1995: 309–343.

An extensive legal analysis on the need for legal protections for gays against hate crimes. Includes much empirical data and an excellent bibliography.

Kifner, John. **". . . And a Racial Shooting."** *New York Times,* December 17, 1995, Section 4: E2.

Soldiers from Fort Bragg, North Carolina, murder two African Americans in a random, racially motivated hate crime.

————. **"Gunman and 7 Others Are Killed as Blaze Guts a Store in Harlem."** *New York Times,* December 9, 1995: 1.

An arson fire at Freddy's Fashion Mart in New York City is partially instigated by antiwhite and anti-Jewish hatred.

"Killing of Gay Resident Stirs Activism in an East Texas Town." *New York Times,* December 27, 1993: A12.

"Klan Member Put to Death in Race Death." *New York Times,* June 6, 1997; A24.

Ku Klux Klan member Henry Francis Hays is convicted of killing an African American youth in Alabama.

"Klanwatch Reports Rise in Hate Crime Activities." *New York Times*, March 5, 1997: A15.

Affiliated with the Southern Poverty Law Center, Klanwatch regularly monitors hate crimes throughout the United States.

Knoll, Erwin. **"A Matter of Intent."** *The Progressive*, August 1993: 4.

This editorial argues that the penalty enhancement provision of hate crime laws will probably be tougher against the same minorities the laws are intended to protect. Also suggests that such legislation may violate freedom of speech.

"Lack of Hate Crimes Coverage Slammed." *Human Rights* (ISSN 0046-8185), Winter 1993: 26–27.

The American Bar Association Governmental Affairs Office sent a letter to the State Department criticizing the lack of coverage of some gay and lesbian issues in its 1991 *Country Reports*. The letter noted the failure to mention the harassment of gay and lesbian rights organizations in Mexico and Argentina.

Lane, Charles. **"The Urge to Outlaw Hate: Germany, America and the Free-Speech Debate."** *Newsweek*, February 15, 1993: 33.

Langer, Elinor. **"The American Neo-Nazi Movement Today."** *Nation*, July 16/23, 1990: 82–108.

Although dated, this is a useful survey of neo-Nazi organizations and individuals.

Lawrence, Charles R. III. **"Crossburning and the Sound of Silence: Antisubordination Theory and the First Amendment."** *Villanova Law Review* 37, 4, 1992: 787–804.

The author, a Stanford University law professor, argues that hate speech harms its victims and undermines "core values in our Constitution."

Lawrence, Christine C. **"Measure Would Increase Hate-Crimes Sentence."** *Congressional Quarterly Weekly Report*, July 31, 1993: 2064.

On July 27, 1993, the U.S. House of Representatives Judiciary Committee approved a measure to increase the length of sentences for hate crimes by one-third. The measure directs the U.S. Sentencing Commission to establish the guidelines for courts.

Lawrence, Frederick M. **"The Punishment of Hate: Toward a Normative Theory of Bias-Motivated Crimes."** *Michigan Law Review*, November 1994: 320–381.

The author, a law professor at the Boston University School of Law, offers the legal justification for hate crimes statutes.

————. **"Resolving the Hate Crimes/Hate Speech Paradox: Punishing Bias Crimes and Protecting Racist Speech."** *Notre Dame Law Review* 68, 4 (1993): 673–721.

A legal analysis of hate speech and hate crimes. Professor Lawrence believes that "bias crime statutes are not only constitutional, they represent the highest expression of a societal commitment to racial, religious, and ethnic harmony."

Leo, John. **"Has Anti-Catholicism Become Acceptable?"** *Reader's Digest*, October 1991: 151–152.

The author claims that gay organizations have mounted a campaign of hate against the Catholic Church that is not reported in the mainstream press.

————. **"A Sensible Judgment on Hate."** *U.S. News and World Report*, July 6, 1992: 25.

Supports the decision of Supreme Court Justice Antonin Scalia, who upheld freedom of speech in the case *R. A. V. v. City of St. Paul*, arguing that individuals cannot be punished for their opinions even if they take the form of a bias-motivated crime.

Levin, Brian. **"A Dream Deferred: The Social and Legal Implications of Hate Crimes in the 1990s."** *Journal of Intergroup Relations*, Fall 1993: 3–27.

This article examines the effects of hate-motivated violence on American society and also discusses the landmark U.S. Supreme Court decision *Wisconsin v. Mitchell*.

Levine, Art. **"The Strange Case of Faked Hate Crimes: An Ugly Form of Fraud Seems to Be on the Rise."** *U.S. News and World Report*, November 3, 1997: 30.

Some individuals have vandalized their own property with hate graffitti for the purpose of collecting insurance and receiving other benefits.

Lieberman, Michael. **"Beating Back the Power of Hate: The Federal Government's Critical Role in Confronting Bias Crime."** *Legal Times,* November 24, 1997:19.

One of the foremost attorneys in the United States litigating in support of hate crime statutes, ADL counsel Michael Lieberman outlines the need for federal government enforcement of these laws.

————. **"Enforcing Hate Crime Laws: Defusing Intergroup Tensions."** *The Police Chief,* October 1994: 18–23.

Lieberman presents the need for law enforcement officials to accurately record hate crime incidents and to prosecute the perpetrators.

MacFadden, Robert D. **"Racial Motive Seen in Attack in Harlem Store."** *New York Times,* December 10, 1995: 1.

An investigative report on the arson attack against a Jewish-owned clothing store in the Harlem section of New York City.

"Man Details How He Ambushed Black Leader in 1980 Shooting." *New York Times,* April 9, 1996: B7.

The neo-Nazi racist Joseph Paul Franklin admits shooting Urban League President Vernon E. Jordan.

"Man Is Acquitted in Doctor's Killing: Prosecutors Called Attack a Bias-Motivated Crime." *New York Times,* May 30, 1993:11.

A racially motivated attack on an Asian Indian medical doctor in Jersey City, New Jersey.

Manatt, Richard W. **"Hate Crimes: Bigotry, Harassment, Vandalism and Violence on Campus."** *International Journal of Educational Reform,* October 1994: 481–490.

This article discusses seven categories of hate crime and focuses on problems affecting students from kindergarten through twelfth grade and also in colleges. Includes a list of resource organizations.

McKenna, Ian B. **"Canada's Hate Propaganda Laws: A Critique."** *Ottawa Law Review/Revue de Droit d'Ottawa* 26,1 (1994): 159–185.

This law journal article analyzes Canadian hate crimes laws, which are much stricter than U.S. statutes.

"The Meaning Of Hate." *National Review,* April 30, 1990: 17.

A critical article on the Hate Crime Statistics Act of 1990.

Mydans, Seth. **"New Unease for Japanese-Americans."** *New York Times,* March 4, 1992: A12.

Japanese Americans have been subjected to recent racial abuse.

Nier, Charles Lewis III. **"Racial Hatred: A Comparative Analysis of Hate Crime Laws of the United States and Germany."** *Dickinson Journal of International Law,* Winter 1995: 241–279.

Examines the rise of hate crimes in Germany and the criminal sanctions instituted both by the United States and German governments to deter such violent crimes.

"No Haven for Hate Crime." *New York Times,* June 16, 1993: A24.

This editorial supports the landmark U.S. Supreme Court decision upholding additional penalties for hate crimes.

Noble, Kenneth R. **"Attacks Against Asian-Americans Are Rising."** *New York Times,* December 13, 1995: B13.

Discusses the upsurge of hate crimes against Asian Americans, especially in northern California.

"Patrols to Fight Anti-Semitic Graffitti." *New York Times,* September 17, 1996: B5.

The New York City suburb of Mamaroneck is plagued with a rash of anti-Jewish vandalism.

Pendo, Elizabeth A. **"Recognizing Violence Against Women: Gender and the Hate Crime Statistics Act."** *Harvard Women's Law Journal,* Spring 1994: 157–183.

An analysis of hate crimes legislation and the need to include gender as a protected category.

Prochnau, Bill. **"The Twisted Tale of a Human Slaughter/ Tragedy in Seattle: A Young Itinerant, His 'Friends' in Outer Space—And**

Brutal Slaying of the Goldmark Family"; "The Shadows of a Killer After the Goldmark Bloodbath: Questions of Motive and Morality." *Washington Post*, May 13 and 14, 1986: C1.

David Lewis Rice killed Charles, Annie, Derek, and Colin Goldmark because he believed the father was Jewish and a communist. Charles Goldmark, a prominent attorney, was neither.

Prutzman, Priscilla. **"Bias-Related Incidents, Hate Crimes, and Conflict Resolution."** *Education and Urban Society*, November 1994: 71–81.

The author discusses how an organization called Children's Creative Response to Conflict is working with teachers and students to teach conflict-resolution skills to reduce bias-related crimes. The article includes recommendations for creating tolerant school environments.

Purdum, Todd S. **"Unhealed Wounds of Crown Heights Bared Again."** *New York Times*, August 12, 1994: B2.

The murder of Jewish scholar Yankel Rosenbaum exposed the rift between the Hasidic and African American communities in the Crown Heights section of Brooklyn, New York.

"Racial Violence Against Asian-Americans." *Harvard Law Review*, June 1993: 1926–1943.

A survey of anti-Asian attitudes and violent incidents directed against Asian Americans in recent years.

Rauch, Jonathan. **"Beyond Oppression."** *The New Republic*, May 10, 1993: 18–21.

The author believes that antigay violence should not be labeled as hate crimes. Although acknowledging that gay-bashing is a problem, he believes that the "oppression model" analysis of gay life is demeaning and counterproductive.

Reinhold, Robert. **"Officials Report Ties of Plotters to Hate Groups."** *New York Times*, July 17, 1993: 6.

White supremacists in Los Angeles, California, are arrested for arming and plotting to start a race war.

Ricks, Ingrid. **"Crying Wolf."** *Advocate* (ISSN 0001-8996), November 29, 1994: 32–36.

A lesbian and her roommates claimed they were victims of malicious vandalism, but further investigations indicated that they attempted fraud to collect on insurance policies.

"The Rise in Hate Crime: Anti-Immigration Policy." *Vital Speeches*, October 1994: 13–16.

A speech by Assistant Attorney General Deval L. Patrick decrying the rise in hate crime against recent U.S. immigrants.

Rosen, Jeffrey. **"Bad Thoughts."** *New Republic*, July 5, 1993: 15–18.

A critical view of *Wisconsin v. Mitchell*, the U.S. Supreme Court decision that upheld hate crime statutes.

Rosenblatt, Roger. **"Their Finest Minute."** *New York Times Magazine*, July 3, 1994: 22.

The inspiring story about the residents of Billings, Montana, who rallied against a rash of anti-Jewish and racist crimes in their community.

Rosenthal, A. M. **"Pogrom in Brooklyn."** *New York Times*, September 3, 1991: A23.

The op-ed columnist discusses the anti-Jewish riots in the Crown Heights section of Brooklyn, New York, which resulted in the death of Yankel Rosenbaum.

Rovella, David E. **"Attack on Hate Crimes Is Enhanced: Critics See Threat to Free Speech as States Stiffen Penalties on Bias-Motivated Crime."** *National Law Journal*, August 29, 1994: A1.

Since the landmark U.S. Supreme Court decision *Wisconsin v. Mitchell*, many states have enacted hate crime laws, bringing the total number to 42.

————. **"Hate Crime Drop Disputed: FBI Reports 1994 Decline, but Watchdog Groups Point to Data Collection Problems."** *National Law Journal*, December 4, 1995: A6.

Sack, Kevin. **"Hate Groups in U.S. Are Growing, Report Says."** *New York Times*, March 3, 1998: A10.

The Intelligence Project of the Southern Poverty Law Center released a report showing a 20 percent rise in the number of extreme right-wing and racist groups throughout the country.

————. "A Son of Alabama Takes on Americans Who Live to Hate." *New York Times*, May 12, 1996: E7.

An interview with Morris Dees, the cofounder of the Southern Poverty Law Center.

"Scalping the Skinheads." *Time*, November 5, 1990: 37.

A civil lawsuit against skinheads involved in murdering an Ethiopian immigrant results in a multimillion dollar settlement and suggests a new tactic to combat hate groups.

Schneider, Keith. "Triple Murder Causes Alarm About Hate Groups' Growth." *New York Times*, March 6, 1995: A1.

Two teenage brothers living near Allentown, Pennsylvania, visited a neo-Nazi compound before committing a triple murder. Sixty-four white supremacist and neo-Nazi groups are active in Pennsylvania.

Seligman, Dan. "The Perfect Crime." *Forbes*, December 15, 1997: 138–139.

Although the Violent Crime Control and Law Enforcement Act of 1994 is often viewed as an important legal weapon against violent white racism, a disproportionate number of blacks commit race-related crimes and are more likely to be prosecuted under this law.

Shalit, Ruth. "Caught in the Act." *New Republic*, July 12, 1993: 12–15.

The author criticizes the Violence Against Women Act of 1993, claiming its broad provisions may violate civil rights.

Shaughnessy, Edward J. "Hate Speech, Bias Crime and the Law." *New York State Bar Journal*, November 1994: 14–17.

This article examines the evolving controversy over hate speech and hate crimes legislation and analyzes pertinent recent U.S. Supreme Court decisions.

Sherman, Rorie. "Abortion Activists Aiding Federal Probe: A Tracking System Based on Klanwatch Was Set Up After the First Doctor Was Killed." *National Law Journal*, August 15, 1994: A9.

The wave of violence against reproductive clinics inspired the Fund for the Feminist Majority's Clinic Watch Program, which is modeled after the Klanwatch program of the Southern Poverty Law Center. The assistant attorney general of the criminal division, Ann Harris, is the head of a task force to investigate the possibility of a national conspiracy to commit violence against these clinics.

Smith, Kyle. **"The Day the Children Died."** *People Weekly,* August 11, 1997: 87–90.

On September 15, 1963, four little girls were killed and 22 others were injured in the bombing of an African American church in Birmingham, Alabama. Although a KKK member was convicted for the murder in 1977, the case is being reopened to possibly find his accomplices.

Solomon, Charlene Marmer. **"Keeping Hate Out of the Workplace."** *Personnel Journal,* July 1992: 30–37.

Addressing human resources professionals, the author discusses how to deal with problems of hate in the workplace. Employees are encouraged to share their feelings and experiences. The employer has the responsibility to ensure that the hiring process is untainted by any forms of racial, religious, or other forms of discrimination. The author singles out the Anti-Defamation League as an important resource organization.

Spillane, Lori A. **"Hate Crimes: Violent Intolerance."** *Prosecutor,* July-August 1995: 20.

The author, a prosecutor in Indiana, argues that members of her profession need to vigorously pursue and prosecute perpetrators of hate crimes.

Stanfield, Rochelle L. **"Leading in a Climate of Intolerance."** *National Journal,* March 14, 1992: 634–636.

To stem the rise of hate and intolerance, the Philip Morris Company, the Ford Foundation, and the Lilly Endowment have invested over $9 million to promote tolerance on college and university campuses. The Southern Poverty Law Center publishes *Teaching Tolerance,* a semiannual magazine, and the Anti-Defamation League sponsors a very successful educational program called A WORLD OF DIFFERENCE.

————. **"The New Faces of Hate."** *National Journal,* June 18, 1994: 1460–1463.

Discusses the rise of bigotry throughout the country, including the anti-Jewish invective of the Nation of Islam, antigay attitudes, and other intolerant views toward minority groups.

Stern, Kenneth S. **"Battling Bigotry on Campus."** *USA Today* magazine, March 1992: 58–63.

Discusses the rise of bigotry on college and university campuses and the role of higher education officials in dealing with this disturbing trend.

"Stiffer Sentences for Hate-Crimes Upheld." *Facts on File,* June 17, 1993: 444–445.

A summary of the U.S. Supreme Court decision in *Wisconsin v. Mitchell* and a related article on the opinion of Chief Justice William H. Rehnquist.

"Supreme Court Overturns 'Hate Speech' Law." *Facts on File,* June 25, 1992: 464–465.

Includes excerpts from the Supreme Court decision in *R. A. V. v. City of St. Paul.*

"Symposium: Stonewall at 25." *Harvard Civil Rights-Civil Liberties Review,* Summer 1994: 283–475.

Most of this issue is devoted to various aspects of gay rights since the police riot at the Stonewall Inn in Greenwich Village occurred on June 27, 1969, marking the beginning of the modern gay rights movement.

Tabor, Mary B. W. **"Police Say Brooklyn Man Faked Bias-Attack Story for Attention."** *New York Times,* January 18, 1992: 26.

Another story indicating the dangers of fabricating hate crime incidents.

Terry, Don. **"Decision Disappoints the Victims of Cross-Burning."** *New York Times,* June 23, 1992: A16.

This story discusses the reactions of Russ and Laura Jones, a black couple from St. Paul, Minnesota, who claimed the criminals who burned a cross on their property committed a hate crime. The U.S. Supreme Court later overturned the local hate crimes statute.

———. **"In Crackdown on Bias, a New Tool."** *New York Times,* June 12, 1993: 8.

Discusses legislative efforts to expand sentences for hate crimes.

Thompson, Elizabeth. **"A Potentially Bloody Red Pages: Access to Watchdog Groups."** *Whole Earth,* Summer 1997: 46–47.

A selective list of organizations that monitor extremist groups and hate crimes.

Van Biema, David. **"Rocky Mountain Hate."** *Time,* December 1, 1997: 53.

Surveys the rash of skinhead violent activities in Denver, Colorado, during the end of 1997.

———. **"When White Makes Right."** *Time,* August 9, 1993: 40–43.

Racist skinheads are considered the most dangerous white supremacist group in the country, with an estimated national membership of 3,500.

Waxman, Barbara Faye. **"Hatred: The Unacknowledged Dimension in Violence Against Disabled People."** *Sexuality and Disability,* Fall 1991: 185–199.

This article argues that disabled people should be a protected category among the groups covered in the Hate Crime Statistics Act of 1990. (As of January 1, 1997, the FBI has been compiling data on this group.) The essay also examines the cultural ideology that leads to violence against disabled people.

Weinstein, James. **"Some Further Thoughts on 'Thought Crimes.'"** *Criminal Justice Ethics,* Summer-Fall 1992: 61–63.

An examination of the pro and con arguments offered by legal scholars on the constitutionality of hate crimes legislation.

Weisburd, Steven B., and Brian Levin. **"On the Basis of Sex: Recognizing Gender-Based Bias Crimes."** *Stanford Law and Policy Review,* Spring 1994: 21–47.

This legal essay examines whether rape and wife-beating should be considered bias crimes.

"When Combating Hate Should Be a Federal Fight." Editorial, *Washington Post*, December 1, 1997: A25.

Critical of the Hate Crimes Prevention Act introduced by Sen. Edward Kennedy (D-MA) and Sen. Arlen Specter (R-PA) in 1997, the editorials claim that law enforcement on these matters should reside with local, not national, officials and that even "ugly intolerance is protected by the First Amendment." Senators Kennedy and Specter explain the need for such legislation.

Winer, Anthony S. **"Hate Crimes, Homosexuals and the Constitution."** *Harvard Civil Rights-Civil Liberties Law Review*, Summer 1994: 387–438.

The author, a law professor, offers the legal and constitutional reasons and provides compelling data to support his view that lesbians and gay men should be covered under existing hate crimes legislation. This essay contains an outstanding bibliography.

Witkin, Gordon, and Jeannye Thornton. **"Pride and Prejudice."** *U.S. News and World Report*, July 15, 1996: 74–77.

Of the estimated 10,000–40,000 hate crimes annually committed in the United States, almost 60 percent of these crimes are perpetrated by youths under 21 years old. Hate speech has also begun to proliferate on the Internet.

Wolfe, Kathi. **"Bashing the Disabled: The New Hate Crime."** *Progressive*, November 1996: 24–28.

Since the passage of the Americans with Disabilities Act, there appears to be a growing backlash against disabled people.The author claims that hate crimes have been committed against the disabled in both low-income and suburban areas.

Zia, Helen. **"Women in Hate Groups."** *Ms. Magazine*, March-April 1991: 20–28.

A survey and analysis of women involved in extremist right-wing and racist organizations.

Reports

The U.S. government, state and municipal entities, and many private organizations publish reports and documents on hate crimes, hate groups, and the growth of bigotry throughout the country. The following selections include some important publications issued in recent years. Although the U.S. government publications should be available in most libraries designated as government depositories, the nongovernmental watchdog organizations must be contacted to obtain their materials. For easier access, U.S. Congressional hearings and reports include the Superintendent of Documents number.

U.S. Government Documents and Reports

U.S. Congress, House Committee on the Judiciary, Subcommittee on Civil and Constitutional Rights, 100th Congress, 1st session (Superintendent of Documents no.: Y4.J89/1:100/116). *Anti-Asian Violence: Hearings, November 10, 1987.*

This hearing examined the causes of and possible responses to recent violent acts committed against Asians and Asian Americans. Witnesses included Rep. Norman Y. Mineta (D-CA); Rep. Robert T. Matsui (D-CA); Floyd D. Shinomura of the Japanese American Citizens League; James C. Tso, president of the Organization of Chinese Americans; and Arthur Soong, president of the Asian American Legal Defense and Education Fund. The report includes a compilation of articles from 1983 to 1987 on violence against Asian immigrants and Asian Americans in Massachusetts and a February 1987 report issued by the Los Angeles County Commission on Human Relations on ethnic- and religious-motivated violence in that region.

U.S. Congress, House Committee on the Judiciary, Subcommittee on Criminal Justice, 99th Congress, 2nd session (Superintendent of Documents no.: Y4.J89/1:99/132). *Anti-Gay Violence: Hearings, October 9, 1986.*

This hearing examined the problem of violence against gay men and lesbians. The report includes descriptions of violent acts, the nature and extent of the violence, and surveys of cultural and social prejudicial attitudes toward gay people. Rep. Barney Frank (D-MA) presented a statement and participated in interviewing witnesses. These included Kevin Berrill, director of the Violence Project of the National Gay and Lesbian Task Force; Dr. Gregory M. Herek, a psychology professor; and Robert J. Johnston, chief of the New York City Police Department. In addition, some gay victims of violence told of their own experiences.

U.S. Congress, House Committee on the Judiciary, Subcommittee on Crime and Criminal Justice, 102nd Congress, 2nd session (Superintendent of Documents no.: Y4.J 89/1:102/80). *Bias Crimes: Hearing, May 11, 1992.*

This hearing focused on crimes motivated by prejudice against the racial, ethnic, religious, or sexual orientation of the victim. The hearing witnesses discussed the Hate Crimes Sentencing Act of 1992, which directs the U.S. Sentencing Commission to revise sentencing guidelines to increase penalties for hate crimes. Witnesses included Rabbi Melvin Burg, whose Los Angeles synagogue was vandalized; Charles J. Hynes, district attorney of Kings County, Brooklyn, New York; and Gary Stoops of the Federal Bureau of Investigation. Other witnesses represented Asian American, Jewish, and gay and women's rights organizations. The report includes the article "Sticks and Stones Can Put You in Jail, But Can Words Increase Your Sentence? Constitutional and Policy Dilemmas for Ethnic Intimidation Laws," by Professor Susan Gellman, published in the *UCLA Law Review,* December 1991 (see earlier entry).

U.S. Congress, House Committee on the Judiciary, Subcommittee on Criminal Justice, 99th Congress, 1st session (Superintendent of Documents no.: Y4.J89/1:99/134). *Crimes Against Religious Practices and Property: Hearings, May 16 and June 19, 1985.*

This hearing discussed a bill to establish federal penalties for damage to any religious building or cemetery and for intimidating any person in the exercise of religious beliefs. Witnesses included Victoria Toensing, deputy assistant attorney general, who objected to the proposed legislation and advocated state, not federal, prosecution of such crimes. Richard Foltin, associate legal director of the American Jewish Committee, testified in support of the legislation.

U.S. Congress, House Committee on the Judiciary, Subcommittee on Civil and Constitutional Rights, 103rd Congress, 1st session (Superintendent of Documents no.: Y4.J 89/1:103/51). *Crimes of Violence Motivated by Gender: Hearing, November 16, 1993.*

Discussed proposed legislation that would make crimes of violence motivated by gender actionable under civil rights and hate crimes laws.

U.S. Congress, House Committee on the Judiciary, Subcommittee on Criminal Justice. 99th Congress, 2nd session (Superintendent of Documents no.: Y4.J89/1:99/135). *Ethnically Motivated Violence Against Arab-Americans: Hearing, July 16, 1986.*

This hearing examined reports of harassment and violence directed against Arab Americans in the United States. Witnesses included Oliver B. Revell III, the executive assistant director of the FBI; David Sadd, executive director of the National Association of Arab Americans; and David M. Gordis, executive vice-president of the American Jewish Committee. The report included testimony of Rep. Mary Oakar (D-OH) and Rep. Nick Joe Rahall (D-WV).

U.S. Congress, House Committee on the Judiciary, Subcommittee on Criminal Justice, 99th Congress, 1st session (Superintendent of Documents no.: Y4.J89/1:99/137). *Hate Crime Statistics Act: Hearing, March 21, 1985.*

The first congressional hearing held to discuss passage of a law to require the U.S. Justice Department to collect and publish statistics on crimes motivated by racial, ethnic, or religious prejudice. Witnesses in support of this legislation included Elaine Jones of the NAACP Legal, Defense, and Education Fund; Jerome Bakst of the Anti-Defamation League of B'nai B'rith; and Rep. Mario Biaggi (D-NY). Opponents of the legislation discussed the anticipated difficulties of determining motivation for certain crimes and the problems of incorporating these statistics into the Uniform Crime Reporting program administered by the U.S. Department of Justice. These witnesses included William M. Baker, assistant director of the Office of Congressional and Public Affairs of the FBI; and Steven R. Schlesinger, director of the Bureau of Justice Statistics. Other witnesses included Rep. Norman Y. Mineta (D-CA) and Rep. Barbara B. Kennelly (D-CN), who testified on crimes of violence against members of ethnic, racial, and religious minorities.

U.S. Congress, House Committee on the Judiciary, Subcommittee on Crime and Criminal Justice, 102nd Congress, 2nd session (Superintendent of Documents no.: Y4:J89/1:102/64). *Hate Crimes Sentencing Enhancement Act of 1992: Hearing, July 29, 1992.*

Discussed the use of penalty enhancement for hate crimes and examined the implications on the constitutionality of hate crime laws following the June 1992 Supreme Court decision *R. A. V. v.*

City of St. Paul, which struck down a Minnesota statute. The following witnesses offered varied views on the constitutionality of the proposed legislation: Professor Laurence H. Tribe of the Harvard University Law School; Floyd Abrams, a prominent constitutional law attorney; Robert S. Peck, legislative counsel of the American Civil Liberties Union; and Susan Gellman, assistant public defender, Ohio Public Defender Commission.

U.S. Congress, House Committee on the Judiciary, 105th Congress, 1st session (Superintendent of Documents no.: Y4.J89/1:105/4). *Implementation of the Church Arson Prevention Act of 1996: Hearings, March 19, 1997.*

This hearing examined the federal agencies' implementation of this act, including provisions clarifying and expanding U.S. federal law enforcement jurisdiction over offenses involving religious property destruction. Witnesses included Patricia C. Glenn, national coordinator of the Church Burning Response Team of the U.S. Department of Justice; Harold McDougall, an NAACP official; and Elder T. Myers, a pastor in a South Carolina church. The report also includes an insertion of the Center for Democratic Renewal's document issued in March 1997, "Fourth Wave: A Continuing Conspiracy to Burn Black Churches."

U.S. Congress, House Committee on the Judiciary, 100th Congress, 2nd session (Superintendent of Documents no.: Y4.J89/1:100/144). *Racially Motivated Violence: Hearing, May 11 and July 12, 1988.*

This hearing considered legislation to establish the Commission on Racially Motivated Violence. The report also examined the prevalence of and responses to acts of violence against members of minority groups and surveyed the history of racial prejudice in the United States and the increase of racial tensions in colleges and universities. Witnesses included Rev. C. T. Vivian, chairman of the Center for Democratic Renewal; Benjamin L. Hooks, executive director of the NAACP; Douglas Seymour, an undercover police agent who infiltrated the Ku Klux Klan in California; and Reginald Wilson, director of the Office of Minority Concerns, American Council on Education.

U.S. Congress, House Committee on National Security, 104th Congress, 2nd session (Superintendent of Documents no.: Y4.Se2/1 A:995–96). *Extremist Activity in the Military: Hearing, June 25, 1996.*

This hearing examined participation of current or former U.S. Army personnel in antigovernment hate groups and militia organizations. It also discussed the murder of an African American couple in Fayetteville, North Carolina, by soldiers of the 82nd Airborne Division based at Fort Bragg, who were affiliated with white supremacist groups.

U.S. Congress, Senate Committee on the Judiciary, 104th Congress, 2nd session (Superintendent of Documents no.: Y4.J 89/2:S.hrg.104–851). *Church Burnings: Hearing, June 27, 1996, on the Federal Response to Recent Incidents of Church Burnings in Predominantly Black Churches Across the South.*

Surveyed the rash of arson against black churches and acts of violence against other houses of worship. Also discussed the federal investigation and prosecution of the perpetrators and financial support to assist in rebuilding the burned buildings.

U.S. Congress, Senate Committee on the Judiciary, 104th Congress, 2nd session (Superintendent of Documents no. Y4.J89/2:S.Hrg 104–842). *Combating Violence Against Women: Hearing, May 15, 1996.*

This hearing examined implementation of the Violence Against Women Act (VAWA) of 1994, providing protection for women against violent crime. Witnesses included Sen. Kay Bailey Hutchinson (R-TX); U.S. Attorney General Janet Reno; Kathryn J. Rogers, executive director of the National Organization for Women (NOW) Legal Defense and Education Fund; and Denise Brown, director of the Nicole Brown Simpson Charitable Foundation.

U.S. Congress, Senate Committee on the Judiciary, 100th Congress, 2nd session (Superintendent of Documents no. Y4.J89/2:S.hrg.100–1069). *Hate Crime Statistics Act of 1988: Hearing, June 21, 1988.*

This hearing considered the proposed legislation to require the U.S. Department of Justice to collect and publish statistics on crimes motivated by racial, ethnic, or religious prejudice. The witnesses endorsing the legislation included Alan M. Schwartz, director of the Research and Evaluation Department of the Anti-Defamation League of B'nai B'rith; Patricia Clark, director of the Klanwatch Project of the Southern Poverty Law Center; Joan C. Weiss, executive director of the National Institute Against Prejudice and Violence; William Yoshino, Midwestern Region director of the Japanese American Citizens League; and Kevin Berrill, director of the Anti-Violence Project of the National Gay and Lesbian Task Force.

U.S. Congress, Senate Committee on the Judiciary, Subcommittee on the Constitution, 102nd Congress, 2nd session (Superintendent of Documents no. Y4.J89/2: S.hrg. 102–1131). *Hate Crimes Statistics Act: Hearing, August 5, 1992.*

Reviewed implementation of the Hate Crime Statistics Act of 1990 by the FBI, state crime reporting agencies, and local law enforcement agencies under the direction of the U.S. Department of Justice. Witnesses included G. Norman Christensen, assistant director of the Criminal Justice Information Services Division of the FBI; Jack McDevitt, coauthor of **Hate Crimes;** and Elsie L. Scott, deputy commissioner of training for the New York City Police Department, representing the National Organization of Black Law Enforcement Executives. Also called to speak were Harold Gershowitz, chairman of the Chicago Regional Board of the Anti-Defamation League; and Elizabeth R. Ouyang, staff attorney for the Asian American Legal Defense and Education Fund, who expressed concern about the possible underreporting of hate crimes against Asian Americans. This report also included the FBI document "Hate Crime Data Collection Guidelines: Uniform Crime Reporting" and the 1991 annual report issued by the Massachusetts Executive Office of Public Safety, entitled "Hate Crime/Hate Incidents in Massachusetts."

U.S. Congress, Senate Committee on the Judiciary, 103rd Congress, 2nd session (Superintendent of Documents no.: Y4. J 89/2: S.hrg. 103–1078). *Hate Crimes Statistics Act: Hearing, June 28, 1994.*

This hearing reviewed the implementation of the Hate Crime Statistics Act of 1990 requiring the FBI to collect and publish statistics on crimes motivated by racial, ethnic, or religious prejudice. The report also examined educational efforts of private organizations to promote tolerance and to prevent hate crimes. One witness was Steven Spielberg, the acclaimed motion picture director and producer, who discussed his perspectives on the making of the award-winning movie *Schindler's List* and its educational value. Other witnesses included Robert Machleder, chairman of the New York Regional Board of the Anti-Defamation League; Sara Bullard, education director of the Southern

Poverty Law Center; and Deedee Corradini, mayor of Salt Lake City, Utah, representing the U.S. Conference of Mayors.

U.S. Congress, Senate Committee on the Judiciary, 104th Congress, 2nd session (Superintendent of Documents no. Y4.J89/2: S.hrg. 104–845). *Reauthorization of the Hate Crime Statistics Act: Hearing, March 19, 1996.*

This hearing considered amending the Hate Crime Statistics Act of 1990 to permanently reauthorize the FBI programs to collect and publish statistics on crimes motivated by race, ethnicity, sexual orientation, disability, or religious prejudice. The witnesses included Charles W. Archer, assistant director of the FBI's Criminal Justice Information Services Division; Emanuel Cleaver II, mayor of Kansas City, Missouri, who represented the U.S. Conference of Mayors; Stephen Arent, vice-chairman of the National Civil Rights Committee of the Anti-Defamation League; and Karen M. Lawson, executive director of the Leadership Conference Education Fund. The report includes the FBI document "Summary Reporting System: National Incident-Based Reporting System; Hate Crime Data Collection Guidelines" and the 1994 Covington and Burlington report "D.C. Bias-Related Crime Act: An Unused Weapon Against Violent Crime," prepared for the Asian Pacific American Bar Association.

U.S. Congress, Senate Committee on the Judiciary, 102nd Congress, 1st session (Superintendent of Documents no. Y4.J89/2:S.hrg. 102–369). *Violence Against Women: Victims of the System; Hearing, April 9, 1991.*

Considered the Violence Against Women Act of 1991, in particular to amend various acts to revise and expand protections against rape and other violent crime. The witnesses included Bonnie J. Campbell, attorney general of Iowa; Roland W. Burris, attorney general of Illinois; and Cass R. Sunstein, a professor at the University of Chicago Law School. The subsequent document includes a committee staff report entitled "Violence Against Women: The Increase of Rape in America, 1990," with tables and graphs.

U.S. Department of Justice, Bureau of Justice Assistance. *A Policymaker's Guide to Hate Crimes,* 1997.

U.S. Department of Justice, Federal Bureau of Investigation. *Training Guide for Hate Crime Data Collection: Uniform Crime Reporting,* 1997.

U.S. Department of Justice, Federal Bureau of Investigation. *Hate Crime Statistics.*

An annual report mandated by the Hate Crime Statistics Act of 1990. The major U.S. government source for assessing the extent of hate crimes nationwide.

Weekly Compilation of Presidential Documents, **"Remarks at the Dedication of Mount Zion A.M.E. Church in Greeleyville, South Carolina,"** June 17, 1996: 1038–1042.

President Clinton promises to prosecute those responsible for the church burnings and to assist communities in rebuilding their houses of worship.

Weekly Compilation of Presidential Documents, **"Statement on the Attack on Jewish Students in Brooklyn, New York, March 2, 1994,"** March 7, 1994: 418.

President Clinton condemns the shooting incident directed against Hasidic Jewish students riding across the Brooklyn Bridge.

State and Municipal Reports

California

California Legislature, Senate Committee on Judiciary. *Interim Hearing on Hate Violence in California: State and Federal Responses to Hate Violence.* Sacramento, CA: Senate Publications, 1993.

Hate Crimes: A Report to the People of San Diego County, 1992–1995.

Considered one of the best and statistically accurate reports on hate crimes published in the United States.

The Ralph and Bane Civil Rights Acts: A Manual for Attorneys. Sacramento, CA: Department of Fair Employment and Housing and the Fair Employment and Housing Commission, 1991.

Representing victims of hate violence in civil proceedings.

Illinois

O'Malley, Jack. *A Prosecutor's Guide to Hate Crime.* Chicago: Cook County State's Attorney's Office, 1994.

Compiled by legal experts, including the ADL Greater Chicago Regional Office, the U.S. Department of Justice, and the Illinois Criminal Justice Information Authority, this handbook provides Illinois prosecutors with a comprehensive approach to understanding hate crimes.

Massachusetts

Harshbarger, Scott. *A Special Report Regarding the Constitutionality of Massachusetts Civil and Criminal Civil Rights Laws.* Boston: Commonwealth of Massachusetts, Office of the Attorney General, 1993.

Massachusetts Governor's Task Force on Hate Crimes. *Hate Crimes in Massachusetts: Annual Report.* (Formerly entitled "Hate Crimes/Hate Incidents in Massachusetts.") Boston, MA: Governor's Task Force on Hate Crimes, 1993– .

Pennsylvania

Five Years of Hate Crimes in Pennsylvania: 1988–1993. Harrisburg, PA: Office of Attorney General and Pennsylvania Human Relations Commission, 1995.

Nongovernment Reports

Nongovernmental organizations and associations have published many major and important studies on hate crimes and extremist organizations. The following list includes the titles of some of these documents. See Chapter 5 for additional information on these organizations and other publications.

Anti-Defamation League

The cost of the following publications vary. Please contact the ADL local or regional branch office or the ADL national office at (212) 885–7700. Some publications can also be obtained from ADL Materials Library, 22-D Hollywood Avenue, Ho-Ho-Kus, NJ 07423; telephone (800) 343–5540; Internet: http://www.adl.org

Addressing Racial and Ethnic Tensions: Combating Hate Crimes in America's Cities (1992).

An American Testament: Letters to the Burned Churches (1997).

Concerned about the burning of churches primarily in the South, the Anti-Defamation League and the National Urban League placed newspaper advertisements in major American newspapers to raise money to rebuild these houses of worship. Many individuals responded with both money and their heartfelt concern; their letters and messages are published in this report. Includes a discussion guide.

Audit of Anti-Semitic Incidents (annual).

Published annually since 1979, this report covers overt acts or expressions of anti-Jewish bigotry and hostility.

Confronting Anti-Semitism: Myths . . . Facts (1997).

This pamphlet explores the origins of anti-Jewish myths and how to counteract them.

Danger: Extremism: The Major Vehicles and Voices on America's Far-Right Fringe (1996).

This 300-page report is the third survey of radical right activity published by the ADL since 1983. An outstanding source, this indispensable document contains profiles of leading individuals and major groups, including skinheads, neo-Nazis, white supremacists, and militias.

Hate Crimes: ADL Blueprint for Action (1997).

A compilation of ADL initiatives, this report was prepared for the November 1997 White House Conference on Hate Crimes.

Hate Crimes Laws: A Comprehensive Guide (1994); *Hate Crimes Laws* (1999).

Essential reports for attorneys, legal scholars, and legislators.

High Tech Hate: Extremist Use of the Internet (1997).

This report states that hate sites are expanding on the Internet, with Holocaust denial the fastest growing anti-Jewish theme. Most of the larger hate groups are now on the World Wide Web, and many of these organizations have learned to use sophisticated technology.

Schooled in Hate, Anti-Semitism on Campus (1997).

Advises appropriate responses needed from college and university administrators, staff, students, and faculty to incidents of anti-Jewish bigotry on campus.

Security for Community Institutions: A Handbook (1992).

Prepared in cooperation with the Crime Prevention Division of the New York City Police Department, this handbook contains a range of practical suggestions and preventive measures that are designed to improve institutional security—including detailed guidance regarding building lighting, restricting access, and emergency procedures.

Center for Democratic Renewal
P.O. Box 50469
Atlanta, GA 30302
(404) 221–0025
Internet: http://www.publiceye.org/pra/cdr/aboutcdr.html

When Hate Groups Come to Town: A Handbook of Model Community Responses (1992).

This manual is frequently cited as an outstanding resource for organizing local community groups.

Southern Poverty Law Center
P. O. Box 2087
Montgomery, AL 36102
(334) 264–0286
Internet: http://www.splcenter.org/

Hate Violence and White Supremacy: A Decade Review, 1980–1990 (1989).

An excellent and useful chronological history that documents the violent activities of white supremacists and neo-Nazis during the 1980s.

Ku Klux Klan: A History of Racism and Violence (1997).

"This hate society was America's first terrorist organization," writes Julian Bond, a veteran civil rights leader. "As we prepare for the 21st century, we need to prepare for the continued presence of the Klan."

The Second Man: Terry Nichols and the Oklahoma City Bombing (1997).

This investigative report covers the activities of Timothy McVeigh's accomplice and also provides an excellent timeline of militia activities and a chart of the so-called Common Law Courts set up by militias and other far right organizations throughout the country.

Nonprint Resources 7

Although most literature on hate crimes and hate groups has been published in books and other print sources, a growing amount of material is now appearing in a nonprint format—including videos, films, and the Internet. This chapter includes information on some of the more useful and important nonprint sources.

Videos and Films

Licensed to Kill
Media type: VHS, 16 mm
Running time: 80 minutes
Release date: 1997
Cost: $295 purchase/inquire about sliding scale price for libraries and community groups.
Distributor: DeepFocus Productions
                 P.O. Box 65095
                 Los Angeles, CA
                 90065–4237
                 (323) 254-7072

In 1977, filmmaker Arthur Dong was attacked by gay bashers on the streets of San Francisco, California. Twenty years later, he produced this film, which contains interviews with imprisoned murderers of gay men. He asks them directly, "Why did you do it?" The film investigates the roots of antigay violence and explores the cultural and social environment of the murderers. The film won the Documentary Director's Award at the 1997 Sundance Film Festival.

Natives: Immigrant Bashing on the Border
Media Type: VHS
Running Time: 25 minutes
Release date: 1993
Cost: $295 purchase/$55 rental
Distributor: Filmakers Library
                124 East 40th Street, Suite 901
                New York, NY 10016
                (212) 808–4980

Portrays the attitudes of some Americans living on the United States–Mexican border, especially their frequently negative feelings toward Mexican Americans and undocumented aliens trying to flee their homeland. One couple advocates machine-gunning down Mexicans after they've illegally crossed the border. The film contrasts the "nativist" reaction of some American citizens to their professed love of the United States and its democratic values.

Pink Triangles: A Study of Prejudice
Against Lesbians and Gay Men
Media type: 16 mm
Running time: 34 minutes
Release date: 1982
Cost: $250 purchase/$50 rental
Distributor: Cambridge Documentary Films
                P.O. Box 390385
                Cambridge, MA 02139
                (617) 484–3993

Although this film specifically deals with the hatred of homosexuals, it is also about the nature of discrimination and the attitudes that provoke violent hate crimes. The film examines historical and contemporary attitudes toward gays and lesbians and the nature of the discrimination they have suffered.

Pockets of Hate
Media type: U-matic/VHS
Release date: 1993

Running time: 26 minutes
Cost: $90 purchase/$25 rental
Distributor: Films for the Humanities and Social Sciences
P.O. Box 2053
Princeton, NJ 08543
(800) 257–5126

Examines the increase in hate crimes and the rise of racist attitudes among some young people.

Who Killed Vincent Chin?
Media type: 16 mm/VHS
Running time: 82 minutes
Release date: 1990
Cost: $395 purchase/$200 rental
Distributor: Filmakers Library
124 East 40th Street, Suite 901
New York, NY 10016
(212) 808–4980

Nominated for an Academy Award, this film portrays the brutal slaying of Vincent Chin, a 27-year-old Chinese American who was killed because of his Asian features. The film discusses the lenient punishment meted out to his assailants and the anti-Asian sentiment that instigated this attack.

Anti-Bias Videos

The Anti-Defamation League is one of the largest producers of human relations materials, including videos, books, teachers' discussion guides, and classroom program activities. The ADL has produced some of the following material; the other films have been released by the film producers listed, and the ADL has agreed to distribute their films and videos. To obtain all the following material, contact:
ADL Materials Library
22-D Hollywood Avenue
Ho-Ho-Kus, NJ 07423
(800) 343–5540
Fax: 1–201–652–1973

Crimes of Hate
Media type: VHS
Running time: 27 minutes

Release date: 1990
Cost: $55/purchase (includes Teacher's
                Discussion Guide)

This video provides an overview of hate crimes in three segments: the crime of racism, the crime of anti-Semitism, and the crime of gay-bashing.

Hate Crimes
Media type: VHS
Running time: 22 minutes
Release date: 1996
Cost: $89 purchase (includes Teacher's
                Discussion Guide)

This program examines the problem of hate crimes, including swastikas on Jewish cemetery tombstones and marches by the Ku Klux Klan. The show interviews both the perpetrators of hate-motivated crimes and the victims.

Learning to Hate
Media type: VHS
Running time: 44 minutes
Release date: 1997
Cost: $90 purchase

Is hatred taught, or does it originate in the family or society? This program focuses on how children learn to hate, and how attitudes toward hatred differ in various cultures. Includes the following segments: an Israeli-Arab youth who becomes a friend of a young Orthodox Jew; high-school students analyzing the origins of hatred against gays and lesbians; and a Holocaust survivor teaching children how stereotypes breed hatred.

Not in Our Town
Media type: VHS
Running time: 27 minutes
Release date: 1995
Cost: $89 purchase (includes Teacher's Discussion
                Guide)
Distributor: The Working Group

This dramatic video documents events in Billings, Montana, after white supremacists victimized Jewish, Native American, and African-American residents. To display solidarity with their Jewish neighbors, residents displayed pictures of a menorah during Hanukkah. The video shows how a community can unite, together battling hatred and violent bigotry.

Not in Our Town II
Media type: VHS
Running time: 58 minutes
Release date: 1996
Cost: $89 purchase

A later look at Billings, Montana, showing the positive effects of the community's unified reaction against hatred. The video also shows other communities that were plagued with hate crimes, church burnings, and other hate-motivated violence and how they fought back.

Videos on Racism and Anti-Semitism

Anti-Semitism on the College Campus
Media type: VHS
Running time: 30 minutes
Release date: 1993
Cost: $55 purchase

This video surveys the reaction of almost a dozen college students to anti-Jewish incidents on their campus.

Ku Klux Klan: The Invisible Empire
Media type: VHS
Running time: 45 minutes
Release date: 1965
Cost: $275

A *CBS Reports* documentary that includes footage of a Klan rally and cross burning and traces the history of this violent racist organization. Also includes interviews with members of the Klan.

Longest Hatred: The History of Anti-Semitism
Media type: VHS
Running time: Three 45-minute segments on two cassettes
Release date: 1991
Cost: unknown

This British three-part documentary surveys "the longest and deepest hatred in human history." Examines the history of anti-Semitism, the present-day situation, and possible methods of combating anti-Jewish hatred.

Other Topics

Hate Crime: A Training Film for Police Officers
Media type: VHS
Running time: 17 minutes
Release date: 1989

Cost: $80 purchase (includes Teacher's Discussion Guide)
This video is designed to train individual police officers in how to properly investigate hate crimes and assist individual victims and the community. Produced in cooperation with the New Jersey Department of Law and Public Safety, this video is useful for law enforcement officials throughout the United States.

Korean Americans
Media type: VHS
Running time: 50 minutes
Release date: 1995
Cost: $149 purchase

This video surveys the Korean American community in Los Angeles, California, featuring discussions with residents and religious and civic leaders. Includes reactions to the recent conflict between African Americans and Korean Americans.

The Anti-Defamation League produces a large number of videos on the subject of diversity and ethnicity, covering groups such as African Americans, Hispanic Americans, and Native Americans, among other minorities. In addition, the ADL is a major source for materials on the Holocaust and interfaith relations. Request the complete catalog, *Anti-Defamation League Material Resource Catalog for Classroom and Community*, at the address listed above.

Internet and the World Wide Web

American Jewish Committee
http://www.ajc.org/

This web site contains information on the programs and activities of the American Jewish Committee (AJC). The pages include material on Israel, interreligious and interethnic activities, Jewish identity, human rights, and combating anti-Semitism and extremism. The founding mission of the AJC is the protection of Jewish rights from extremist and anti-Semitic attack, and the site provides much useful material on these programs, including Hands Across Campus, which promotes student understanding of America's multicultural and multiethnic society. The pages titled "Combating Anti-Semitism and Extremism" describe the AJC's efforts to counter bigots and neo-Nazis involved in the Holocaust denial movement, the pernicious effects of "Hate Talk on Radio," and organizational efforts to support hate crimes legislation. The site also includes an extensive annotated list of publications covering anti-Jewish attitudes and activities in the United States and throughout the world. Nicely designed and extremely informative, this site is an important resource to learn about the malignant growth of anti-Jewish hate.

Anti-Defamation League (ADL)
http://www.adl.org/

The web site of the largest organization in the world combating anti-Semitism, *ADL Online* is an outstanding source of information for students, researchers, and the concerned layperson. (The "ADL Search" link expedites your search of the site.) The full text or summaries of some ADL print publications now appear on this site, including the indispensable legal guide, *1999 Hate Crimes Laws; The San Diego Hate Crimes Registry;* and *Schooled in Hate: Anti-Semitism on Campus.* In addition, the site contains ADL Model Crime Penalty Enhancement Laws. Other pages contain:

- Information on how to report anti-Jewish incidents;
- The programs of the WORLD OF DIFFERENCE Institute to strengthen pluralism in the United States and advance diversity education;
- Summaries of several fact-finding reports, including *Beyond the Bombing: The Militia Menace Grows; ADL Anti-Paramilitary Training Statute: A Response to Domestic Terrorism; Holocaust Denial: An Online Guide; Skinhead International: A Worldwide Survey of Neo-Nazi Skinheads;* and *High Tech Hate: Extremist Use of the Internet;*
- The *ADL Material Resource Catalog for the Classroom and Community,* containing summaries of the print, audio-visual, posters, magazines, and other materials produced or distributed by the ADL.

• *Frontline*—Current and past issues of *ADL on the Frontline,* the national newsletter of the Anti-Defamation League.
• The latest annual report of the ADL.

Center for Democratic Renewal
http://www.publiceye.org/pra/cdr/cdr.html

The Center for Democratic Renewal's web site includes the full text of the CDR report *The Fourth Wave: A Continuing Conspiracy to Burn Black Churches;* excerpts from the CDR book *When Hate Groups Come to Town;* "Ten Tips for Fighting Hate Groups of the Far Right"; current and back issues of *CDR Activist,* which surveys the activities of hate groups throughout the world; and selected CDR reports, including the *Christian Identity Movement.*

Coalition for Human Dignity Information Center
http://www.chd-seattle.org/chd/

This web site includes discussion of the goals and projects of the CHD (see Chapter 5), and current and back issues of the CHD quarterly newsletter, *Dignity,* which includes excerpts from previous editions organized topically. These include the attack on Temple Beth Israel in Eugene, Oregon, in 1994 and the activities of James "Bo" Gritz and his allies in the neo-Nazi and Christian Identity movement in Idaho. Topical reports are also accessible, including *The Northwest Imperative: Documenting a Decade of Hate,* which surveys white supremacist activities in the Pacific Northwest over a three-year period, and excerpts from *When Hate Groups Come to Town.*

Federal Bureau of Investigation
http://www.fbi.gov/ucr/ucreports.htm

This web site provides data on bias-motivated criminal incidents with breakdowns by race, religion, sexual orientation, and ethnicity/national origin. As of January 1, 1997, disability bias crimes have been included. The offense categories included in the collection of hate crime data are murder and nonnegligent manslaughter, forcible rape, robbery, aggravated assault, burglary, larceny-theft, motor vehicle theft, arson, simple assault, intimidation, and destruction/damage/vandalism to property.

Hatewatch
http://www.hatewatch.org

Originally posted as a Harvard University library guide entitled "A Guide to Hate Groups on the Internet," the site soon grew too large for the library web page and expanded to its own site in 1997. Hatewatch is a private, not-for-profit organization and has no affiliation with Harvard University. The organization has a small staff and volunteers throughout the world. Although Hatewatch does not advocate censoring hate groups or hate speech, the web site "strongly recommends Internet Search Providers (ISP) and Web space providers voluntarily have a 'no hate page policy' as part of their users' terms of service contract." The founder, David Goldman, has assembled an outstanding site for monitoring the growing presence of hate groups on the Internet.

Leadership Conference Education Fund Online
http://www.lccr.org/lcef/hate/toc.html

Sponsored by the Leadership Conference on Civil Rights, the nation's oldest, largest, and most diverse coalition of civil rights organizations—now numbering more than 180 groups—the Leadership Conference web site contains the full-text of the report *Cause for Concern: Hate Crimes in America.* Also useful is a page of links (http://www.lccr.org/lcef/hatelinks.html) that provide easy access to the FBI hate crimes report, the Anti-Defamation League, and many other useful sources.

National Gay and Lesbian Task Force
http://www.ngltf.org/

The NGLTF web site includes a map of hate crime laws in the United States, noting states that specify crimes based on sexual orientation, and a search site that will retrieve relevant press releases and other documents. A keyword search on "violence" or "hate crimes" will yield much useful material.

New York City Gay and Lesbian Anti-Violence Project
http://www.avp.org/

This web site provides much useful information on reporting hate crimes, articles on antigay violence, and research on the effects of these crimes on their victims. The site contains the text of the *NCAVP Annual Report* (National Coalition of Anti-Violence Programs), which documents the extent of antigay violence throughout the United States. The report attempts to rectify the underreporting of these incidents to law enforcement agencies. In addition, the site includes addresses and phone numbers of antigay violence programs throughout the United States and a list of publications, brochures, and posters.

Nizkor Project

http://www.nizkor.org

This site, named after the Hebrew word for "we will remember," contains extensive information on the history of the Holocaust, including information on concentration camps, the transcripts of the Nuremberg War Crimes Tribunal, and other historical documents. The site also publicizes the activities of neo-Nazis and other Holocaust deniers (often misleadingly referred to as "revisionists") and attempts to counter their hate in electronic forums, principally the Internet. Ken McVay, a non-Jew, established the site because he was appalled at the dissemination of anti-Jewish material on the Internet.

Northwest Coalition Against Malicious Harassment

http://www.nwb.net/nwc/

This web site includes back issues of the coalition's quarterly newsletter *Northwest Beacon*. The site contains an "Anti-Bias Education Resource Guide Summary" of state laws in the region (including Colorado, Idaho, Montana, Oregon, Washington, and Wyoming) regarding malicious harassment—the term this organization uses for bias crimes.

Political Research Associates

http://www.publiceye.org/

This is a graphically pleasing and well-organized web site that includes an extensive range of information: documentation and analysis of right-wing conspiracy theories; excerpts from racist, anti-Jewish, and antigay publications; a list of publications, topical reports, bibliographies, and reading lists; current and back issues of the *Public Eye,* the PRA quarterly newsletter; and the full text of an important 1994 report by Chip Berlet, senior PRA analyst, entitled *Right Woos Left*—an analysis of the burgeoning alliance between both ends of the political spectrum on issues ranging from the Gulf War to the CIA.

Simon Wiesenthal Center

http://www.wiesenthal.com/

This web site provides information on the activities of the Simon Wiesenthal Center, an international institute for Holocaust remembrance and the defense of human rights for the Jewish people and other groups. The pages include a calendar of events and membership information; current issues of *Response,* the organizational newsletter with a circulation of more than 300,000; information on the Museum of Intolerance and a calendar of events and exhibits; international documents about the organization in several languages, including Spanish, French, German, Italian, Japanese, and Swedish; *Cyberwatch Survey,* created to determine the "degree of understanding and level of concern Internet users have regarding the use of the Information Highway by groups and individuals to promote bigotry and hatred"; *Cyberwatch Hotline,* which allows users to report incidents of anti-Semitism, racism, or other forms of bigotry; and information on the Holocaust and black-Jewish relations.

Southern Poverty Law Center
http://www.splcenter.org

This site contains information on the activities of the center and its affiliate, Klanwatch. Available are *Intelligence Report,* a quarterly newsletter that profiles extremist groups and monitors domestic terrorism; press releases, news articles, and numerous links to other pertinent literature on hate-motivated violence and hate groups; classroom resources, including how to order *Shadow of Hate: A History of Intolerance in America,* a 40-minute video with a 128-page illustrated text, *Us and Them.*

Stephen Roth Institute for the Study of Contemporary Anti-Semitism and Racism
http://www.tau.ac.il:81/Anti-Semitism/index.html

The Project's web site contains excerpts from *Anti-Semitism Worldwide,* an annual report that surveys and analyzes anti-Jewish activities throughout the world. Source material comes from individuals and institutes, the media, and government ministries, as well as Jewish communities and organizations. Also available is a recent chronology of anti-Jewish activities around the world. The site provides a detailed description of the Wiener Library in Tel Aviv, Israel, and contact information for the Wiener Library Reading Room.

Vidal Sassoon International Center for the Study of Anti-Semitism
http://www6.huji.ac.il/~www_jcd/.index.html

Established in 1982 as an interdisciplinary research center dedicated to an independent, nonpolitical approach for understanding the phenomenon of anti-Semitism, the center engages in research on anti-Semitism throughout the ages, particularly situations of tension and crisis. Its web site was started in 1994 and includes an easy-to-use home page that guides the user to both summary and full-text materials, including the Analysis of Current Trends in Anti-Semitism research report on anti-Jewish trends in various countries throughout the world. An outstanding collection of links to other sites on anti-Jewish attitudes and activities and other forms of bigotry is provided. The site lists a bibliography of studies on anti-Semitism and includes an informative essay by Professor Shmuel Almog on the spelling and use of the term "anti-Semitism." Also available are the center's annual report and back issues of its newsletter.

Users also may access the Felix Posen Bibliographic Project on Antisemitism, an on-line database of works published throughout the world about anti-Semitism, including books, dissertations, and articles from periodicals and anthologies. (It doesn't include book reviews, newspaper articles, or anti-Jewish publications.)

Index

D onald Altschiller is a librarian at Boston University. He has edited several books and his articles have appeared in major national newspapers. A reviewer of reference books for library journals, he has also contributed essays in several encyclopedias, including ABC-CLIO's *Historical Encyclopedia of World Slavery.*